Queer Joints, Wiseguys and G-Men

PHILLIP CRAWFORD JR.

CONTENTS

Introduction — i

1 Baltimore Mayor D'Alesandro Protected Mafia Vice Rackets — 1

2 FBI Director Hoover Killed Mafia Commission Investigation — 19

3 Philadelphia Mafia Bosses Operated Maggio Cheese Company — 33

4 Gay Mob Associate Headed Boy Toy Crew — 48

5 FBI Agents Investigated Jack Ruby For Gay Ties — 58

6 Germano Crime Family Operated Albany Gay Bars — 64

7 1962 Clampdown On Rochester Gay Bars — 74

8 Buffalo Movie Theater Was Gay Cruising Ground — 81

9 Gay Bar Hopping Across The USA — 88

INTRODUCTION

From 2009 to 2019 I wrote the blog *Friends of Ours* about the Mafia. After a decade I quit blogging in order to focus on writing books and other projects, and rather than keeping a dormant blog online I deleted it. However, several posts from my blog contained original research involving FBI files obtained pursuant to the Freedom of Information Act, and to ensure their continued availability as historic resources have collected them in this book.

Many of these slightly reworked posts involve gay bars, Italian mobsters and FBI agents and their crossing paths from the late 1950s into the early 1960s. Included among them are the following tales: Baltimore mayor Thomas D'Alesandro – the father of U.S. House Speaker Nancy Pelosi – was corrupted by the Mafia, and provided protection for its vice rackets; FBI Director J. Edgar Hoover ignored an early warning about the Mafia Commission which allowed organized crime to spread its tentacles across the United States; Texas mayor Sam Hoover was a mob associate who ran a burglary crew of teen boys which doubled as his stud stable; and Jack Ruby had extensive ties to the gay scene – and may have been homosexual – which the FBI investigated after he shot JFK assassin Lee

Harvey Oswald. The book also includes gay bar hopping adventures across the country in the pre-Stonewall era compiled from FBI files which had identified "notorious places of amusement" in its extensive surveys of local crime conditions.

I am a pre-Stonewall baby. The Stonewall riots in June 1969 mark the beginning of the modern gay rights movement. In the pre-Stonewall years LGBT folks had no legal rights, and they assembled through a bar subculture. Of course, those bars often had a precarious existence, and the fate of the Ekim Bar on the Upper West Side in New York City which was shut down in 1961 – the year of my birth – was typical.

The Ekim Bar at 2696 Broadway and 103rd Street had been owned by Michael J. Freeman since 1934, and experienced many incarnations over the decades. For example, during the 1950s it was known as the Ekim Calypso Dock serving Italian cuisine, and booked acts including Gene Vincent and his Calypso Troubadours and Kert DePass and his Queen Bee. By the early 1960s it was a hot spot for the gay scene, and on September 30, 1961 an alleged hustler was busted there by Detective Vincent Leonardo from the 24th Precinct according to court records involving an enforcement proceeding by the Liquor Authority.

The detective entered the Ekim Bar at 2:05 a.m. in plain clothes – "I was wearing a checked suit, brown and white; also a brown tie, white shirt, horn-rimmed glasses, and a hat, a beaver hat as they call them, which is more or less on the style of a homburg" he testified – and the place was hopping. Detective Leonardo testified there were about one hundred men and "one apparent female," and "the majority of the patrons, in my opinion, were homosexuals." Asked how he could tell the patrons were homosexuals, Detective Leonardo stated they were "talking in high pitched voices that would, if I hadn't seen a person speaking, I would surmise it was a female," and "I also heard some of the patrons refer to other patrons in the premises as 'Darling,' 'Deary.'"

Detective Leonardo testified that he observed gay action immediately upon siding up to the bar:

At that time, directly to my left, there were two males, unknown males, actually. At that time one unknown male walked over to these two unknown males and he was introduced to the one unknown male seated at the bar. One was introduced as "Betty" and the other as "Lois." They engaged each other in conversation. After a short period of time they proceeded to fondle one another. They then kissed on the lips for a prolonged period of time. Subsequently, they kissed some more. At about 2:15 they left the premises in each other's company.

Apparently the detective was such a hot number that two patrons – identified as Gerald and Gregory – could not keep their hands off him once he took a seat at the bar, and Leonardo testified as follows:

He [Gerald] kissed me upon the ear a number of times. He fondled my private parts, placed his hands upon my buttocks, and used endearing expressions to me. Also seated to my left, at that time, was an unknown male known to me only as Gregory. This Gregory engaged me in conversation. He fondled my private parts and placed his hand upon my buttocks and rubbed my buttocks. At various times either Gerald or this Gregory would place his hand on the small of my back and rub the small of my back.

Gregory was an Italian boy, and he won the day in vying for Detective Leonardo's affections after allegedly offering to service him – "I can suck your prick" – for ten bucks, and upon leaving together the ungrateful copper arrested him:

He then started to leave the bar and he said, "Come on." He left the bar and I was immediately behind him. I said to him, then, "Where are we going?" Prior to leaving the bar he had said to me, he said, "We can't go up my place because my friend is up there." I said, "What's the difference?" He said, "My friend is up there turning a trick." I said, "Oh." He said, "Do you have a place to go?" I said, "No, I'm staying with some friends in town and I can't go there." Then we left and once outside he said, "Listen, do you have a place to go?" I said, "No. I told you 'No,' I can't go any place that I know of." He repeated that his friend was "turning a trick" in the apartment with someone else. He said, "We'll go to Central Park." We started to walk and I then placed him under arrest.

Gregory was criminally prosecuted on a Section 887-4C charge which prohibits loitering for the purpose of committing a lewd and indecent act but thankfully he was acquitted by the trial judge in Magistrates' Court. However, the Liquor Authority nevertheless revoked the liquor license for Ekim Bar as a disorderly premise catering to homosexuals.

Several years later on a weekend in June 1969 the LGBT community fought against police harassment outside the Stonewall Inn. At that time I was just a little boy spending the summer with my family in a rented cottage at Higgins Beach in Scarborough, Maine, and knew nothing about that auspicious event as it unfolded in Greenwich Village. Although

I was acutely aware even as a 7-year-old that I liked boys I had no word for the desire, and "homosexual" was not yet in my vocabulary. However, the shame of that identity already was instilled within me, and I was suffering in isolation with my secret. Just a decade later the liberating momentum from the Stonewall riots had reached even Bates College in Lewiston, Maine at which I matriculated in September 1980.

I was in the closet throughout high school, and had no intention of remaining in that suffocating place in college. My freshman year I attended a forum sponsored by the Gay-Straight Alliance which had formed only a year or two earlier, and I was captivated by stories about "gay ghettos" in cities such as Boston and New York. The GSA had only a few members and met infrequently, and in my sophomore year was ready to disband. The loss of the group would be the loss of my community, and at that time it was the only vehicle through which I was able to express my identity. It was time for me to come out to the world, and in order to continue the GSA I stepped forward as its new President for the academic year 1982-1983 during which I was a junior.

The GSA under my leadership increased its campus visibility including a campaign to ban military recruiters for their discriminatory policies. In the early 1980s LGBT rights were few. On March 2, 1983 about 25 GSA members staged a sit-in at the Bates College career center where Marine recruiters met with straight students who were curious about a military path. The previous month both the college administration and student government had rejected a GSA proposal to ban the military recruiters. The sit-in received extensive media coverage including a prominent feature by Louis Berney for *The Boston Globe*. After all, as noted by Berney, if Bates enacted such a prohibition it would "become the first undergraduate college in the country to do so," and at that time only a handful of law schools already had enacted such a ban due to the military's discrimination against homosexuals.

The campus response to the GSA campaign to ban military recruiters involved cynical sophistry and reactionary ugliness. For example, the Dean's Office issued a public statement rationalizing the military's presence by extolling the need for competing ideas while conveniently ignoring that the recruitment activity involved a positive act which offered a real opportunity only for straight students while denying it to gay ones:

> We will continue our policy of allowing all organizations, including the military, to recruit

on campus. It is not, in our estimation, appropriate for us to preclude individual students from interviewing with military recruiters if they wish, nor is it appropriate for us to impose our own beliefs about sexual preference on an outside agency. This would be contrary to our adherence to the principle that the college is an open forum where ideas and beliefs, no matter how much at variance with our own, can be freely represented.

In short, Bates College advanced discrimination under the guise of open debate. And in reaction to the GSA an Alliance of Straight People was launched which reportedly promised that the entire football team dressed in camouflage fatigues would counter-protest any gay sit-in against the military recruiters.

Although the GSA campaign to ban military recruiters was unsuccessful, nearly thirty years later in 2011 Congress lifted the ban against gays and lesbians from openly serving in the military. In 2015 President Barack Obama nominated out defense official Eric K. Fanning to become Secretary of the Army. Tony Kushner writes in *Angels in America* that "the world only spins forward." However, in 1983 at Bates College most people were trying to stall its rotation.

At the time of the Stonewall riots in June 1969

many gay bars were controlled by the Mafia because of their illicit status. There was a direct correlation between LGBT oppression and our underworld existence, and so community connections often formed in Mafia dives. Just as queer rights were not immediately achieved after a weekend fight at the Stonewall Inn, the Mafia did not suddenly relinquish its control over gay bars. Indeed, in 1983 when I became GSA President at Bates College, Genovese capo Matty Ianniello – one of the hidden owners of the Stonewall Inn – still controlled many gay watering holes in New York.

In the early 1980s when I came out the drinking age was only 18-years-old, and over the next decade I hit the gay bars along the Northeast Corridor from Boston to New York to Washington, D.C. Many establishments were dark and seedy, and known for backroom sex, drug dealers and rough trade. A few times I naively wondered how do these places get away with all this? Only years later did I learn that organized crime ran many gay bars, and as a general rule the business model for the mob-tied ones included illicit activity on the premises whereas legitimate places were operated by the book. Over time as the LGBT community gained rights the prevalence of Mafia bars diminished as our acceptance into polite society allowed for respectable establishments. These days with victories such as marriage equality the mob's role in gay bars surely is nearly eliminated. But as with any fight surely there is more work to do.

1 BALTIMORE MAYOR D'ALESANDRO PROTECTED MAFIA VICE RACKETS

United States House Speaker Nancy Pelosi often recounts learning about politics as a little girl during the 1950s when her father Thomas D'Alesandro Jr. ran the Democratic machine in Baltimore, Maryland. D'Alesandro was a Congressman for five terms from 1938 to 1947, and Baltimore mayor for three terms from 1947 to 1959. The Honorable D'Alesandro allegedly was a "constant companion" of notorious mobster Benjamin "Benny Trotta" Magliano and other underworld figures according to the FBI file on the old-school politician. The mob ties and other corruption allegations against Mayor D'Alesandro curiously have remained absent in the accounts by Speaker Pelosi about her political family.

In 1947 the FBI investigated Benjamin Magliano for securing a draft exemption from Selective Service for himself and prize fighters he controlled by falsely representing they had essential employment at American Ship Cleaning Company which was operated by John Cataneo. In fact, Magliano and his boxers had no such employment, and they were convicted with Cataneo in federal court for their unpatriotic draft-dodging scam. Peter Galiano, one of the convicted boxers, told the FBI in January 1947 that "Thomas D'Alesandro was a constant companion of John Cataneo; Benjamin Magliano . . . and [redacted]":

> It was reported that these individuals had worked hard for Thomas D'Alesandro's reelection to Congress and on his campaign at that time to become Mayor of Baltimore. It was stated that John Cataneo and Magliano during the time of this campaign were under Federal indictments for violation of the Selective Service Act and for fraud against the Government and were subsequently convicted in Federal court. Cataneo allegedly admitted giving large sums of money toward the Democratic campaign and stated that he would receive the sanitation contracts for Baltimore if Mr. D'Alesandro was elected mayor.

At that time the FBI never investigated D'Alesandro concerning this or numerous other allegations involving hoodlum associations and public corruption.

Of course, D'Alesandro sat on the appropriations committee in the U.S. House of Representatives, and once pointedly told a supervisory special agent that he had backed the Bureau and Director J. Edgar Hoover perhaps as a reminder not to bite the hand that feeds them. An FBI memo dated March 27, 1946 from E. G. Fitch to D. M. Ladd provides:

> Supervisor Orrin H. Bartlett advised me that while talking to Congressman Thomas D'Alesandro, Jr. (D., Md.) on March 26, 1946, the Congressman advised Agent Bartlett he was running for Congress again in the fall 1946 election and that in 1947 he was running for the office of Mayor of Baltimore. Congressman D'Alesandro advised Agent Bartlett that since he had been on the Appropriations Committee, he has been backer of the Director and the Bureau one hundred percent, and further, that he was vitally interested in and completely satisfied with the results of the Bureau's work.

Hoover sent warm congratulations to D'Alesandro upon his November 1946 re-election to the House and then his May 1947 election as Baltimore Mayor, and after leaving Congress for City Hall D'Alesandro wrote Hoover by letter dated May 14, 1947:

> Thank you very much for message congratulating me on my election as Mayor of the City of Baltimore. I was most pleased to receive your good wishes and assure you that I will do my utmost to give the people of Baltimore an efficient and outstanding administration. I, too, will miss you and many other friends in Washington but I am grateful for the proximity of our two cities which will afford the opportunity for frequent visits when and if time permits. Whenever you are in Baltimore, please make it a point to visit me at City Hall.

Meanwhile, the corruption allegations against D'Alesandro continued to pile up.

Finally, in January 1961 President John F. Kennedy requested that the G-men investigate "allegations of D'Alesandro's involvement with Baltimore hoodlums; with favoritism in awarding city contracts; [and] protection for political contributors and the prosecution of local cases." President Kennedy wanted to appoint D'Alesandro to the United States Renegotiation Board which was a government watchdog against profit gouging by defense contractors. A February 6, 1961 memo from

Hoover to the Baltimore and Washington Field Offices cautiously advises: "The White House has requested that we proceed with a special inquiry investigation but that if substantial derogatory information were developed, we should report this and discontinue any further inquiries because substantiation of any of the allegations would eliminate D'Alesandro."

The FBI inquiry was a perfunctory exercise with little digging which vainly attempted to address two decades of allegations in less than two months, and of course some witnesses had lost their memories and others had died or otherwise disappeared. For example, Peter Galiano, the convicted boxer involved with Magliano's draft-dodging scheme had told Special Agent James V. Sullivan in January 1947 that D'Alesandro was a "constant companion" of both Magliano and Cataneo. However, more than a decade later, on February 8, 1961 Galiano told the FBI that his original statement was "only rumor and hearsay," and "he could not recall who gave him this information or whether or not there was any truth to these allegations." Nevertheless, there was independent corroboration for at least some of Galiano's earlier allegations. The FBI notes that "during the investigation" of the Selective Service fraud case "SA JAMES V. SULLIVAN had occasion to be at the American Shipcleaning Company Offices in Baltimore on a number of occasions and had seen appointee [D'Alesandro] in the company of JOHN CATANEO." Moreover, Special Agent Sullivan in 1947 had received from another informant "similar information" concerning D'Alesandro's ties to both Cataneo and Magliano, and this informant further advised that "CATANEO also supposedly was well-regarded by D'ALESANDRO because he had control of a large Italian vote in Baltimore."

D'Alesandro also was accused by highly-credible police officers of providing protection to Baltimore hoodlums. For example, "in 1945, Captain JOHN R. ROLLMAN, Western District, Baltimore Police Department, Baltimore, Maryland, furnished information to the Baltimore Office of the Federal Bureau of Investigation concerning one CHARLES F. CAMMARATA, who until a short time previously had operated a tavern at 641 West Baltimore Street." According to Captain Rollman "CAMMARATA had gotten away with all sorts of criminal activities in the Western District due to the protection of Maryland United States Representative THOMAS D'ALESANDRO," and "CAMMARATA was alleged to be gambling in various crap and card games in Baltimore." Once again, the FBI never did anything about these allegations at the time they were made, and by 1961 when the G-men finally got around to looking into them Captain Rollman had died and "CAMMARATA's current whereabouts are unknown." A March 15, 1961 FBI memo reports that Cammarata may have been last seen in Havana, Cuba in the mid-1950s where he allegedly "had some connection with Clark's Tropicana Night Club," and now may be residing in Miami, Florida where he "reportedly owned apartment houses"; however, perhaps content to let sleeping dogs lie, the FBI never followed up on these tips in an attempt to reach Cammarata about the alleged protection he received from D'Alesandro while operating in Baltimore.

The flesh trade in Baltimore during the 1950s ranged from harmless burlesque shows to sinister child prostitution, and much of it operated on "the Block" according to an August 1959 FBI report. The report states that "'the Block' is generally considered a section of East Baltimore Street between Holliday and North High Streets, 400 to 900 block east" which allegedly was controlled in some measure by Benjamin Magliano under the protection of Mayor D'Alesandro. The FBI stated "for a number of years 'The Block' has been the location of a number of low-class night spots where strip tease performers are featured, 'B-girls' solicit drinks and prostitutes ply their trade." Thomas D'Alesandro lived with his family in Little Italy at 245 Albemarle Street just a few blocks directly south of "the Block," and was fully aware of its goings-on.

The FBI identified the following as vice dens in "the Block": Ringside Bar at Albemarle Street; Shot Tower Bar at North High Street; Benny's Bar at 826 East Baltimore Street; Harry Corral Bar at 515 East Baltimore Street; Club Diamond near Harrison Street; Village Bar at North Harrison Street; Crystal Bar at 417 East Baltimore Street; Flamingo Bar at 503 East Baltimore Street; Gayety Nite Club at Custom House Avenue; Gay White Way at 10 North Gay Street; Galley Bar at 626 East Baltimore Street; Club Troc at 400 East Baltimore Street; Miami Nite Club at Frederick Street; Villanova Nite Club at 418 East Baltimore Street; Florida Bar at 608 East Baltimore Street; 408 Club at 408 East Baltimore Street; Oasis Nite Club at Frederick Street; and Kay's Club at Frederick Street.

According to the August 1959 FBI report "merchant seamen, sailors and civilians frequent the above places regularly," and "it is alleged that people from Washington come to Baltimore in order to enjoy the entertainment in this area." The FBI characterized the "entertainment" as follows:

Customers in these places are solicited by the "B-Girls" to purchase drinks. If the customer seems friendly, he is then propositioned by the girls for a "date." The approach of the girls is very direct in most instances. They generally will name the time for the date and the place where the date will take place. Generally the girls will take the customer to her own apartment nearby or possibly to a nearby low-class hotel. The 408 Club and the Gay White Way have the greatest number of prostitutes frequenting the premises. Generally these girls will go from one club to another, depending on how business is at the various spots. Generally the girls in this area receive $20.00 for a date but recently the price obtained has decreased to $10 to $15.00. The girls have learned that "things are tough."

At least three of the clubs on "The Block" – The Troc, Club 704, and The Gay White Way – allegedly had direct ties to Benjamin Magliano a/k/a Benny Trotta. The FBI described The Troc as "a notorious night spot on "the Block" where "strip-tease dancers are featured," and "the dances are described as 'a real good strip.'" Moreover, "private shows have been put on for customers in the dancer's dressing room after the scheduled show," and "the dancers are generally expected to associate with the customers between shows to get them to buy more drinks" and "the dancers are also expected to further entertain patrons away from the club." Benny Trotta was identified as the owner and operator of The Troc, and "is generally at the side door during the evening and night hours greeting customers." Benny Trotta reportedly also was a hidden owner of Club 704 which was managed by Hitty Wildstein who was related to him by marriage, and The Gay White Way which was operated by his son-in-law Angelo Munafo. The FBI described The Gay White Way as "frequented by prostitutes and female sitters," and "girls frequenting this place have reportedly rolled customers after obtaining dates at this bar."

Although much of Charm City's vice activity was on East Baltimore Street there also was action on West Baltimore Street, and the August 1959 FBI report alleges the following:

> The other night clubs located on West Baltimore Street also catering to prostitutes include the Copa Night Club located at 21 West Baltimore Street, which has regular strip tease shows. Known prostitutes frequent this bar. Other places in this area catering to prostitutes are Frank's Bar, 676 West Baltimore Street, and El Dorado Lounge, 322 West Baltimore Street.

The North Charles Street area also was a hot spot

for working girls according to the same report:

> Prostitutes who formerly frequented "The Block" are reportedly currently frequenting the Blue Mirror on North Charles Street. The Baltimore Sun Newspaper of March 13, 1959, reported that a patrolman from The Baltimore City Police Department testified before the Liquor Board that shady characters are frequenting the Charles Street area near Mount Royal Avenue. He referred to many of the saloon patrons as prostitutes and confidence men looking for prospects to roll.

According to the patrolman some of the prostitutes working North Charles Street were as young as thirteen:

> He continued that teen-aged girls from 13 on up practice prostitution in that area, aided by youths serving as procurers. The Flying Saucer, a restaurant near the Bandbox on North Charles Street is a hangout for teen-aged drapes and the type of teenager who wears motor cycle jackets. Teen-aged girls who hang out in this area are being prostituted.

Benjamin Magliano a/k/a Benny Trotta allegedly owned the Star Attraction on North Charles Street which the FBI characterized as a booking agency providing girls "for strip shows" and "for immoral purposes for individuals who desired them."

In addition to the vice dens "the Block" also had "cheap movie houses and cheap hotels," and "there are tattoo parlors, flop houses, and novelty stores in the area." The August 1959 FBI report alleged that "BENNY TROTTA owns the premises at 402 E. Baltimore Street on 'the Block,' which adjoins the Troc," and "he rents this property to an individual who operates a novelty shop on the premises."

Of course, no red-light district is complete without smut shops. According to the FBI report the Block included "three large bookstores which prominently display large quantities of literature having suggestive titles and covers," and "also display numerous magazines bearing photographs of nudes." The FBI identified the smut shops as follows: Lloyd's Bookstore at 409 East Baltimore Street; Corner Bookstore at 427 East Baltimore Street; and Ben Siegel's Bookstore at 428 East Baltimore Street.

Lesbian bars also were located in "the Block." An "official investigation in December, 1957" involving "physical surveillances and interviews of patrons of certain taverns in the City of Baltimore . . . developed the information that the following taverns are notorious as 'hangouts' of Lesbians": Cicero's Cafe on Forrest Street between Gay and

Ensor Street; Mary's Cafe at Fleet and Washington Streets; Rally Club at Forrest and Ensor Streets; and Yorktowne Bar at 2200 Block East Monument Street. The FBI further noted that "several bars have been identified in Baltimore as being hangouts for homosexuals," and "the most commonly known such hangout is Cicero's Night Club on Forest Street across from the Bel Air Market." The "girls frequenting Cicero's are known to be Lesbians," and Cicero's apparently also was a clip joint because "girls at this place are paid $5.00 a night as employees and receive a commission of $.25 on drinks bought for them by customers." Many bars which offered safe haven to gays and lesbians in the 1950s particularly in smaller cities also involved other sexual outlaws where prostitutes or B-girl hustled desperate men.

Benjamin Magliano a/k/a Benny Trotta was identified by the FBI as one of Baltimore's "top hoodlums," and widely was acknowledged as the representative for New York's Frankie Carbo (born Paolo Corbo). Carbo was responsible for multiple murders with Murder, Inc., and he later became a made guy in the Lucchese family. The FBI in a 1958 report said "CARBO reportedly a member of the crime syndicate in New York City, and to control the boxing racket" and he "controls many fighters through other managers of record, recently [redacted name] and [redacted name] in New York City" and "fixes fights for gambling benefit and has been reported to control various crap games and bookmaking." By at least 1953 Carbo was expanding the vice rackets for the Lucchese family down the east coast, and "it was reported his New York mob was taking over prostitution, 'junk' traffic, gambling, and bookmaking in Miami, Florida." In 1958 Carbo was living at 2637 Taft Street in Hollywood, Florida according to FBI records.

In addition to mob ties Mayor D'Alesandro faced multiple charges of public corruption including an allegation that he had received kickbacks from building developer Dominic Piracci on city contracts. Piracci's account ledger included several payments totaling $11,000 to D'Alesandro which he later erased to keep the information from investigators. The developer explained that the payments were legitimate loans to Mrs. D'Alesandro to finance her cosmetics business which since had been fully repaid, and he doctored the documents only "to save" the D'Alesandro family "from embarrassment and from further trouble" given a criminal investigation into his business practices. In April 1954 Piracci "was found guilty of conspiracy to defraud the city of $42,996 in connection with the construction of an off-street parking garage in Baltimore," and also found guilty for "obstruction of justice in that he submitted to a Baltimore City Grand Jury a 'completely phony' ledger to conceal $35,000 in weekly payments to the Peoples Holding Corporation" whose officers "were also charged with conspiracy to defraud Baltimore City in an off-street parking garage contract." Mrs. D'Alesandro testified on Piracci's behalf at his criminal trial, and although she insisted the "loans" from Piracci were repaid there was no documentary evidence to corroborate that testimony. The supposed repayments were made in cash rather than by check. Mrs. D'Alesandro's testimony may have saved her husband's sorry ass from criminal liability but could not save his then-bid to become Maryland's governor. The D'Alesandro's son Thomas III later married Piracci's daughter Margaret.

The Piracci trial at which Mrs. D'Alesandro testified immediately was followed by a child gang rape trial against the Mayor's 20-year-old son Franklin Roosevelt D'Alesandro. The FBI describes the ugly case in a January 30, 1961 memo as follows:

> During the summer of 1953, Mayor D'Alesandro's son, Franklin Roosevelt D'Alesandro, aged twenty, was one of fourteen youths charged with having committed rape or

perverted practices on two girls, aged eleven and thirteen, during July of that year. It was reported that Franklin Roosevelt D'Alesandro was the only one of twelve of those tried at that time who was successful in obtaining an acquittal. Following this acquittal, a Baltimore, Maryland, Grand Jury indicted Franklin Roosevelt D'Alesandro on charges of having committed perjury in that he had lied during the aforementioned trial on charges of rape. In addition, James H. Pollack, Baltimore City political boss, was reportedly also indicted on the charge of obstruction of justice in that he had attempted to influence testimony of several of the youthful defendants who had been tried with Franklin Roosevelt D'Alesandro. It was reported that Franklin Roosevelt D'Alesandro was tried on the above charge of perjury at Salisbury, Maryland, during 1954, following a change of venue, and was found not guilty.

The FBI notes in a February 27, 1961 memo that according to one informant "the consensus of opinion among persons connected with law enforcement that appointee's [D'Alesandro's] son acquitted of rape because of brilliant fashion case handled by defense attorney." Franklin Roosevelt D'Alesandro was represented by Joseph Sherbow who managed to sever his client from the other defendants and ensured his trial went first so any convictions against the others would not prejudice him. Apparently Mayor D'Alesandro believed that his son was guilty of the charge, and prior to trial urged him to plead guilty and "take his medicine."

The corruption charges and his son's rape trial had become more than Mayor D'Alesandro could bear, and he suffered a nervous breakdown. D'Alesandro was admitted to the Bon Secours Hospital in Maryland where he rested from March 10 through July 12, 1954. During this period according to an FBI memo "the Baltimore City Police Department had two men assigned to protect the appointee [D'Alesandro] and also had two men guarding his home" at 245 Albemarle Street for unknown reasons and "a local paper carried a picture of him in his hospital room seated in front of a television set, dressed in a dressing gown."

Most of the FBI's "special inquiry" into D'Alesandro involved brief interviews with his political cronies, personal friends and family members who insisted the Mayor was a swell guy. The allegations against D'Alesandro involving public graft and hoodlum associations were conveniently ignored or gratuitously explained away, and on March 28, 1961 he was sworn in as a member of the

United States Renegotiation Board by President Kennedy. D'Alesandro's wife and their 21-year-old daughter Nancy were by his side.

2 FBI DIRECTOR HOOVER KILLED MAFIA COMMISSION INVESTIGATION

On November 14, 1957 state troopers raided the home of Joseph Barbara in Apalachin, NY where Italian crime bosses from across the country were meeting, and the following year the FBI released its so-called Mafia Monograph officially recognizing "available evidence shows that beyond the shadow of a doubt, the Mafia does exist today in the United States, as well as in Sicily and Italy, as a vicious, evil, and tyrannical form of organized criminality." However, more than two decades earlier in 1935 a former Army intelligence officer specifically warned the Bureau that a national syndicate based in Brooklyn, New York governed Italian gangs throughout the United States. The national syndicate at issue likely was the Mafia Commission established in 1931 by Lucky Luciano, and J. Edgar Hoover was personally apprised of its existence in a pair of "personal and confidential" letters from the Special Agent in Charge of the New York Field Office. Inexplicably, the Director refused to authorize his men to further investigate it.

Al Capone was convicted on federal tax evasion charges in 1931 and sentenced to ten years in prison, and in 1935 Major Charles E. Russell, a former officer within the intelligence unit of the Army in Europe during World War I, advised the FBI's New York Field Office that the imprisoned gangster's Chicago operations now were being run out of Brooklyn by a national syndicate which further took a cut from mob rackets in all other cities.

R. Whitley, the Special Agent in Charge at the New York Field Office, relayed Major Russell's revelations directly to J. Edgar Hoover in a "personal and confidential" letter dated August 3, 1935:

Major Russell stated that the headquarters of the Al Capone syndicate have been shifted from Chicago to Brooklyn, and that the entire racket syndicate field, including vice, gambling, liquor and various other lines, is now controlled and directed by a man named Vito and two men named Totto of Brooklyn. They have associated with them many notorious racketeers, including

"Dutch" Schultz, and the three men are the heads of the syndicate. At their headquarters they have a group of young men, none of whom appear to be over twenty-four years of age, who are professional killers and whose activities are limited to performing that function for the syndicate. They have numerous henchmen, including young lawyers, doctors, and various other men of the professional type, as well as the usual gangster type. They receive a "cut" from all the racketeer operations from Chicago to the east coast and from Boston to below Philadelphia.

Of particular concern to the FBI was Major Russell's claim that this governing board was seeking to infiltrate the Department of Justice for counterintelligence purposes, and Whitley advises Hoover in the August 3 letter: "he [Major Russell] stated that he was told by these underworld characters that they have available men who can meet all the requirements for appointment to a position in the Department."

In a second "personal and confidential" letter dated September 10, 1935 Whitley further advises Hoover that "the present headquarters of the so-called Capone Syndicate, controlling racketeering in the Middle West and East, is located in Brooklyn,

N.Y., near the Brooklyn Navy Yard." More specifically:

> He [Major Russell] made a rough diagram showing the Lane Democratic Club on York Street, and stated that this is a hangout for some of the minor members of the organization; that two of the so-called "big shots" live on York Street; one of them, known to him as "Mike," lives on the same side of the street as the Lane Democratic Club is located and a block or so south, while another one, known to him as "Charlie," lives on the opposite side of the street some distance north of the location of the Lane Democratic Club. The Lane Democratic Club is located at about the middle of the block, and according to Major Russell, the actual headquarters of the Syndicate is located in the premises occupied by an ice cream parlor on either one of the two streets between which the Lane Democratic Club is located and at the corner of the street east of Sands Street and parallel thereto. * * * Major Russell also stated that a favorite hangout for these people is in a grill or cafe, the name of which is the "Seashell" or some similar name.

The FBI visited the locations described by Major Russell, and surmised that the ice cream place to which he referred was Nassau Ice Cream Parlor at the corner of Gold and Nassau Streets, and the eatery was the Sea Grill at the corner of North Elliott Street and Flushing Avenue.

The purpose of the national syndicate was to allocate territories and resolve disputes according to Major Russell as Whitley relayed to Hoover in the September 10 letter:

> As to the operations of these people, Major Russell stated that as far as he knows, these men do not themselves participate in any activities such as handling "hot" bonds or jewelry or operating any vice or gambling establishments. They do, however, completely control the so-called "protection" racket. They have divided the entire Middle West and East into districts, and the City of New York is also divided into districts, and the people operating in the various criminal activities in these districts do so with the permission of the Syndicate and in accordance with the dictates of the Syndicate. Disputes between various operators of illegal activities in the districts, or disputes between contiguous districts are settled by this Syndicate, and practically daily meetings are held by the heads of the Syndicate in the premises in which the above-mentioned ice cream parlor is located. It

is impossible to operate any of the profitable rackets without the sanction of this Syndicate, and the revenue of the Syndicate is derived from the cut which it takes on all revenue from such activities.

The operational description provided by Major Russell for this national syndicate sounds spot on like the Mafia Commission created only years earlier by Lucky Luciano after the 1931 hits on Joe Masseria and Salvatore Maranzano which ended the Castellammarese War. The "Vito" to whom Major Russell refers may be Vito Genovese who in 1935 was the underboss to Luciano, and the two "Tottos" may be brothers Generoso Del Duca (1896-1960) and Pasquale Del Duca (1890-1964), both nicknamed "Toto" or "Toddo," who were Genovese family members out of South Brooklyn. Generoso was a capo who died of a heart attack in the arms of Frank Sinatra after a night of clubbing in Miami, Florida with the crooner and Joseph "Joe Fish" Fischetti who was a first cousin of Al Capone and worked alongside the Chicago gangster.

The credibility of Major Russell's claims is underscored by his allegation that the Chicago operations were run by this national syndicate out of Brooklyn. Johnny Torrio – Capone's predecessor and mentor in Chicago – in fact had returned to

New York after the Capone trial, and was one of the principal advocates to Luciano for the Mafia Commission. Major Russell may not have been quite right with all his underlying facts in describing the Mafia Commission but it is clear he was onto the more fundamental truth of its existence, and may have been the first to so advise the FBI.

Whitley concluded his September 10 letter to Hoover by stating that "no further investigation is being undertaken with reference to the activities of the Syndicate described by Major Russell, pending receipt of instructions from the Bureau." Inexplicably, no further instructions ever were forthcoming from the Director on the matter.

The warning from Major Russell that the national syndicate employed well-educated professionals and was well-positioned to infiltrate the Department of Justice was well-founded. Organized crime cannot exist without public corruption, and the Mafia operated legitimate fronts and nurtured respectable connections. An early example of the Mafia's role in legitimate affairs through which it possibly could attempt to compromise the Justice Department involved a Brooklyn federal prosecutor who co-owned Brunswick Laundry Service with mobster Joe Bonanno.

Among the legitimate businesses owned by Mafia boss Joseph Bonanno was Brunswick Laundry Service at 39-45 Central Avenue in Brooklyn. The business was incorporated in 1932, and FBI documents reveal that the mobster acquired his interest supposedly by strong-arming its founding shareholders including Vincenzo Passalacqua who was the father of Assistant U.S. Attorney Peter Anthony Passalacqua for the Eastern District of New York. Incredibly, AUSA Passalacqua at one time was a shareholder and officer of Brunswick Laundry Service, and fully aware of Bonanno's involvement in the company. Indeed, Peter Passalacqua admitted to FBI agents that while in private practice before becoming a federal prosecutor he prepared at his father's request in 1939 or 1940 the "legal papers in connection with the transfer of 1/5 of the shares of stock in the above corporation to JOSEPH BONANNO," and "it was on this occasion that he first met BONANNO."

The FBI interviewed AUSA Passalacqua on November 27, 1957, and according to FBI documents "he said that his father told him that BONANNO was being given 1/5 of an interest in the corporation so that there would be no union trouble in the laundry or so that the trucks of the laundry would be permitted to 'roll' without interference by anyone." After Bonanno was given his 1/5 interest in 1939 or 1940, Vincenzo then transferred his own 1/5 interest to Peter:

PASSALACQUA said that in approximately 1941 or 1942 his father transferred his 1/5 interest to him. He explained that this transfer was made at this time inasmuch as his father was suffering from cataracts in both of his eyes and he felt his son PETER should have this stock in his name. PASSALACQUA added that the stock was thereupon transferred into his name and in approximately 1945 or 1946 after a successful operation on the cataracts of his father's eyes the stock was again transferred back to his father. PASSALACQUA said that during the time he held the stock in his name, he believed he was listed as an officer on the corporation books, however, he stated that he never acted in that capacity inasmuch as he never took an active part in the business nor did he attend any meetings.

With the assistance of a "Sicilian speaking agent" the FBI interviewed AUSA Passalacqua's father Vincenzo at his home on 97 Stanhope Street in Brooklyn on January 15, 1958, and Vincenzo detailed how Bonanno allegedly acquired an interest in the company:

PASSALACQUA related that he was an original share holder of Brunswick Laundry Service, Inc., 41 Central Avenue, Brooklyn. He asserted that prior to World War II, a truck was stolen from Brunswick Laundry and was missing for a number of hours. He said JOSEPH BONANNO appeared on the premises of the Laundry and offered to recover the truck, which he did. At that time, BONANNO approached a stockholder and offered to guarantee no more trouble in connection with other trucks being stolen, if he was placed on the payroll at $25 per week with payments being rendered BONANNO to BONANNO's brother-in-law (name unknown) each Friday.

The weekly $25 payoff from Brunswick Laundry to Joseph Bonanno continued for "approximately four years," and then in a typical greedy mob move the boss upped the ante and wanted to get a further hold over the company through an ownership interest:

BONANNO approached officials of the Laundry relative to securing one-fifth share of stock of the Laundry, and offered in return a guarantee that the Laundry will have no trouble with unions, racketeers, or anyone.

PASSALACQUA said that BONANNO asserted that this was necessary, in order that it would appear to authorities that he, BONANNO, derived legitimate income from the Laundry. Officials of Laundry agreed and BONANNO was given one-fifth interest. PASSALACQUA said that the $25 payments to BONANNO were not given to him until the weekly payments aggregated the value of the one-fifth interest. PASSALACQUA advised that at that time, BONANNO demanded that officials of the Laundry increase his weekly payments to $45. Officials agreed and the $45 payments were made to BONANNO and are being made at this time. These payments are still being collected on Fridays by BONANNO's brother-in-law. According to PASSALACQUA, BONANNO has never worked for or at the Laundry in any capacity.

The FBI quickly determined that Bonanno's brother-in-law was Joseph Spadaro, and after putting him under surveillance apparently substantiated Passalacqua's allegations. At the end of January 1958 the FBI discussed the case with the U.S. Attorney Cornelius Wickersham for the Eastern District of New York who determined that Brunswick Laundry Service was an extortion victim under the Hobbs

Act but declined prosecution against the mob boss in order to "not impair the development of other information concerning the subject."

Although the FBI officially had recognized the Mafia in 1958, even by 1960 Director Hoover still had his personal doubts. A March 23, 1960 memo from the Director to the Miami Field Office pursuant to which he authorized the illegal bugging of Meyer Lansky states the following:

> You now have residing in your territory one of the very most important individuals in the national crime picture in the person of Meyer Lansky. Information developed in Bureau investigations over a period of many years indicates strongly that Lansky is a very important individual in a segment of the criminal element. In pursuing investigations in your Criminal Intelligence Program, you should not overlook the possibility of employing extraordinary investigative techniques with reference to Lansky. Because of the loss of the lucrative Cuban gambling situation, Lansky is presently in a position of having to make decisions as to his future course of action. This may be a propitious time for close coverage of Lansky.

However, the memo further reflects Hoover's lingering questions about the very existence of the

Mafia, and its relationship to non-Italians such as Lansky. Already contemplating the distinction between a made member who must be Italian and a mob associate who can be of any ethnicity Hoover writes:

> It is desired also to point out to you the need of continuous alertness to develop the existence or nonexistence of the "Mafia." Persons who furnish information in this field should be thoroughly interviewed for a determination of what they mean by the use of the term "Mafia." It is the Bureau's desire to determine whether or not this is a mere term used to characterize criminal groups made up of a preponderance of persons of Italian birth or extraction, or whether it is a term denoting something of greater significance. Complete details of any facts available should be obtained from any persons contending that it is an actual organization which can be characterized as being a "Mafia."

The FBI's ignorance about the Mafia decades after its entrenchment in the United States was astounding. For example, Assistant Director Louis Nichols – Hoover's No. 2 man – left the FBI in 1957, and took a plum job making $100,000 a year at Schenley Industries which mob lackey Roy Cohn allegedly secured for him, and Louis Rosensteil, the company's president, was suspected of ties to Genovese mobsters Meyer Lansky and Frank Costello. The failure of Hoover to authorize further instructions to investigate the 1935 allegations of a national syndicate governing the Italian crews throughout the United States no doubt was a missed opportunity to nip the Mafia in the bud, and perhaps constitutes the FBI's biggest intelligence failure in its otherwise storied history.

3 PHILADELPHIA MAFIA BOSSES OPERATED MAGGIO CHEESE COMPANY

The brilliance of the Mafia not only was its involvement with criminal schemes but its immersion in legitimate businesses even if they often operated through illegal means or used as distracting fronts behind which nefarious activities were conducted. For years Michael Maggio used his cheese company on 11th and Washington Streets in Philadelphia, Pennsylvania as Mafia headquarters, and after his 1959 death his protégé Angelo Bruno continued operating the crime family's numbers and loansharking rackets out of it.

In August 1958 the FBI characterized Maggio as the "retired chairman of the Board" of the Greaser Gang and "retired head of the 'Mafia' in Philadelphia" who was "old and in bad health" but "still contacted concerning policy matters by Greaser

Gang and other groups." One informant "advised that MAGGIO is one of the top men in the Greaser Gang with connections all over the United States as well as in Italy, that he was born in Sicily and is a member of the Mafia," and another informant "has reported that MAGGIO is one of the big men in the Mafia who has committed many murders and whose word goes far."

On July 26, 1958 "MAGGIO was interviewed at his residence by Bureau Agents" at 2519 South 21st Street, and "MAGGIO was receptive to an interview and talked at length concerning his legitimate enterprise, the Maggio Cheese Company of Philadelphia." Maggio "admitted knowing" a number of local racketeers about whom the FBI asked including Angelo Bruno, Dominick Pollina, Peter Casella, Felix de Tullio, Phil Testa and Salvatore Falcone; however, "MAGGIO states that he associates with these individuals only as a result of business that comes up with the Maggio Cheese Company," and "MAGGIO denied that he ever engaged in any illegal activities."

According to the FBI Angelo Bruno's home was in the neighborhood of the Maggio Cheese Company, and he "spends considerable time there." The FBI confirmed through IRS and other records that Dominick Pollina was a Maggio Cheese employee, and listed as a Vice President. One informant told the FBI that Pollina "actually uses that position as a front and office for a loan sharking business." According to another informant "POLLINA has a large amount of money, most of which he has made by loan sharking," and is "personally a physical coward unless he has strong arm men to back him up, but that with help, POLLINA will not hesitate to slap around any person who is slow in repaying loans."

A January 1958 FBI memo makes the following assessment about business operations for Maggio Cheese:

On December 16, 1957, Confidential Informant T-34 said that M. Maggio Cheese Company, with plants on the southwest corner of 11th and Washington Streets, 916-18 South 9th Street, and 903-11 Montrose Street, was organized by MICHAEL MAGGIO in 1920. MICHAEL is the president; [name redacted]; Peter J. MAGGIO, secretary, and [name redacted]. The financial condition of the company is listed as sound with turnover of assets normal or better. The company was chartered on October 14, 1946, with capital stock of $50,000. The Milkmaid Dairy Products, Inc., and the Vineland Cheese Company, Inc., both of 759 South East

Boulevard, Vineland, N.J., occasionally sell to the M. Maggio Cheese Company. PETER J. MAGGIO is president of Milkmaid and secretary of the Vineland Cheese Company. The M. Maggio Cheese Company employs an average of 25 persons, including six driver-salesmen and sells in the Philadelphia area. Business is located in a one-story brick building at 11th and Washington which is owned by the officers and rented to the corporation. It has a branch in Denton, Md., which is a receiving station for milk. The property on South 9th and Montrose Streets belong to the corporation and have a combined value of $27,300.

In March 1958 the FBI determined that "the Maggio Cheese Company maintains a bank account at the Broad Street Trust Company in Philadelphia, and the members of the firm, who are all members of the MAGGIO family, also have accounts there," and "the firm's account shows frequent withdrawals by check in three and four figures." FBI "inquiries during the week of 3/3/58 at Penn Fruit Stores Company, Food Fair Stores, and Acme Stores, reflect that M. Maggio Cheese Company does business with these concerns, averaging approximately $7,000 or better per year."

Maggio Cheese Company did not always

compete fairly in the legitimate economy during the time mobster Michael Maggio was its president according to an FBI informant in a 1958 report. An informant identified as T-2 alleged Maggio Cheese was not the best but its product nevertheless was "sold in the Philadelphia area in all of the large chain stores and in a great many independent neighborhood grocery shops" due in some instances to extortionate practices by mob goons:

On January 27, 1958, T-2 reported that MAGGIO has a monopoly on the Italian cheese business in the Philadelphia area although the best Italian cheese is made by a man named [redacted] who has a grocery store in South Philadelphia. [Name redacted], however, is permitted to make only enough cheese to sell in his own store. Sometime ago [name redacted] told T-2 that PETER CASELLA sent men into his store who smashed it up and told him that he would be killed if he did not stop trying to compete with the Maggio Cheese Company. Since that time he has restricted his manufacture. T-2 also said that one [name redacted] operates a [redacted] establishment on [redacted] in South Philadelphia and that he made arrangements to buy another brand of cheese than Maggio to use in his establishment. He was soon visited by representatives of Maggio whom T-2 did not identify and told him that he would be killed if he did not buy Maggio Cheese. He now buys it.

Philadelphia mobsters often doubled as sales representatives, and query whether Maggio Cheese was the only company which used high-pressured tactics. Felix "Skinny Razor" DeTullio whom Maggio admitted knowing through the cheese business once held down two account representative positions for different companies at the same time according to a March 1958 FBI report. The report provides that "on November 6, 1957, FELIX JOHN DE TULLIO was interviewed by the Philadelphia Police Department," and the mobster produced multiple business cards including one which identified him as an "account representative" for C. Vilotti Bakery at 615 Fitzwater Street, and another which identified him as a salesman for Queen Beverage Company at 824 South Fifth Street.

The operator for C. Vilotti Bakery advised the FBI on February 10, 1958 that "he has known SKINNY (FELIX DE TULLIO) for about 20 years," and "DE TULLIO approached him in the summer of 1956 for employment as an account representative and was hired at a salary of about $60.00 per week." The Vilotti Bakery was "primarily wholesale, selling to institutions, restaurants, retail stores and bakeries with about ten per cent of the sales retail," and "net sales for the calendar year 1956 amounted to $245,000."

In addition to selling cannoli, DeTullio also sold booze. The FBI confirmed DeTullio's employment with Queen Beverage Company on February 6, 1958 which apparently had hired him six years earlier "as a salesman, primarily on a wholesale basis" at a pay rate of "$75.00 per week as long as DE TULLIO's sales grossed at least $1,500 per week, a quota which DE TULLIO was always able to sell." The company "named the following places that were customers of DE TULLIO": Freddie's Bar at Pine Street and Delaware Avenue; Streets of Paris Cafe at 216 South 11th Street; Flannigan's Bar at 3 North 13th Street; Buckeye AA at 1226 South 8th Street; and Flamingo Cafe at 54th Street and Woodland Avenue. DeTullio allegedly was the hidden owner of the Television Bar at 1039 South 8th Street which was fronted by Alfred Iezzi. Iezzi "formerly operated the Ticket Grill at 1304 Wharton Street from 1941 to 1945," and "many sources reported this latter bar as a racket hangout."

Michael Maggio apparently retired in late 1955 "due to age and ill health," and business operations were turned over to his son Peter. Michael Maggio wintered in Miami where mobsters including Angelo

Bruno frequently visited him but Maggio often returned to Philadelphia, and he drove a Florida-licensed 1958 cream colored four-door Cadillac sedan. Michael Maggio's health continued to deteriorate, and in February 1959 he was at Temple University Hospital in Philadelphia "where he had a very serious operation." He was "released from the hospital in a very poor condition" by early March 1959, and "it was felt that MAGGIO probably had a malignant condition and due to his age was not given too long to live." On "being released from the hospital MAGGIO was immediately taken to his winter home in Miami Beach, Fla. by his son [name redacted]."

Michael Maggio died in Miami Beach on March 14, and "his body was returned to Philadelphia for viewing on 3/18/59, and burial on 3/19/59." Two FBI "informants were present at the viewing and state that 'everybody who is anybody in the business' was there to show their respect":

Both informants estimated several thousand persons attended the viewing and both stated they understood the funeral procession contained at least 20 or 30 flower cars. They said this large funeral would indicate the position MAGGIO held in the criminal world. [Redacted] said that in his opinion, because of MAGGIO's age and physical condition, the turnout was for MAGGIO's influence in the past when he had been more active and not for any recent activity. One informant "advised that ANGELO BRUNO attended the funeral of MICHAEL MAGGIO, mentioned above," and "the informant said that BRUNO told him he made the trip from Miami specifically to attend the funeral and was going to return immediately to Miami after the funeral as he was seriously considering making Miami his permanent home."

This same "informant also advised that with the death of MICHAEL MAGGIO, BRUNO is probably now considered the 'Mahoff' of the Italian criminal element, in the Philadelphia area." A September 1959 FBI report alleges "ANGELO BRUNO has been increasingly mentioned as the Philadelphia leader of the Italian racketeers," and "when in Philadelphia ANGELO BRUNO uses the offices of the Maggio Cheese Company as his headquarters." A confidential informant advised the FBI that "'a lot of numbers action' was going into the Maggio Cheese Company at the present time," and "the Maggio Cheese Company is the location of BRUNO's numbers bank." Moreover, loan shark Dominick Pollina still "is employed by instant company located at 11th Street and Washington

Avenue, Philadelphia, which is also a known hangout of BRUNO." On December 12, 1959 special agents "observed a 1950 Buick, Pennsylvania registration L 05458 at the Maggio Cheese Company which is registered to IGNAZIO DENARO who is known to most informants as a leading loan shark in Philadelphia."

The loansharking and numbers rackets were lucrative enterprises for Bruno and Pollina. An FBI informant alleged the following about loan sharking by Angelo Bruno in a 1958 report:

> On January 20, 1958, T-2 said that he had known ANGELO BRUNO, a member of the Greaser Mob, for a long time and knows him to be extremely wealthy. He said BRUNO is active in lending large amounts of money to racketeers and is reported to have made big loans to various members of the Jewish Mob and in this manner to have financed them in many of their activities. T-2 said that although the racketeers who borrow the money may be wealthy, they prefer not to borrow money for illegal ventures from banks but rather from other racketeers knowing that in this way the transaction can be concealed from the Internal Revenue Service.

Informant T-2 also "has reported that DOMINICK POLLINA is the wealthiest loan shark in the

Philadelphia area and has had many persons beaten for their failure to repay his loans," and Pollina "has at least four men working for him in his money lending operations which furnished his income, his position at the Maggio Cheese Company being only for the record."

Although "no definite information has ever been received in Philadelphia to indicate that the Greaser Gang was engaged in the narcotics traffic as a group," some FBI sources speculated that Angelo Bruno was the financial backer for Peter Casella who was arrested on January 23, 1958 for violation of the Federal Narcotics Laws. The informant "theorized that with the large amount of narcotics purchased and their tremendous value CASELLA had to have financial backing because it has been known for several years that he was in poor financial condition and had borrowed large sums of money," and the informant "suspected that ANGELO BRUNO may have furnished some of the funds" because "BRUNO is wealthy and is known as a loan shark." This same informant "also expressed the opinion that if CASELLA were released on bond he might be killed by the Greaser Gang for having bungled his narcotics venture" but "there was a possibility that CASELLA's close personal friendship with BRUNO might save him." Casella was convicted in 1959 for narcotics, and spent close to the next twenty years behind bars.

The FBI advised the IRS "of BRUNO's [alleged] numbers bank location" on December 9, 1959, and an IRS Philadelphia section chief "states he intends, based on this information, to use approximately a six man force to establish the existence of a gambling (numbers) operation at the Maggio Cheese Company with the objective of arresting BRUNO, POLLINA and others for not possession a federal gambling stamp." Although the IRS official "says this would be a weak case for prosecution in federal court . . . a search incidental to arrest would be made hoping to locate records, money or any material for possible prosecution." By January 21, 1960 "agents of the Internal Revenue Service are now conducting an audit of the books of the Maggio Cheese Company formerly owned by MICHAEL MAGGIO, deceased, and presently controlled by the MAGGIO sons," and although "this cheese company is known to be a hangout of ANGELO BRUNO and he is reported to maintain an office there" since "the Internal Revenue agents have been auditing the books, BRUNO has not been around and he is supposed to be out of town."

Philadelphia government was notoriously corrupt, and the numbers and loansharking business operated by Maggio and Bruno thrived due to their payoffs. An informant dubbed T-23 whom the FBI characterized as "active in Philadelphia and Pennsylvania politics for many years" advised on February 24, 1958 "that in his opinion there is a tie-up between the criminal element of the City of Philadelphia and the political representatives," and "he bases this conclusion upon what he personally has observed and the information related to him by various persons":

> T-23 stated that many of the office holders in the present City Government are dishonest, either in those instances where they take "tips" in order to expedite the handling of various documents such as leases, court orders or motions, or else in those fields where they dishonestly use their power in order to decide matters of a penal nature. In the latter category, he cited the police officers, building inspectors, employees of the Weights and Measures Department as the more prevalent violators.

The FBI informant provided specific details about dirty cops in the "red cars" who took bribes to provide protection for the numbers racket: "[H]e stated that he believes Commissioner of Police THOMAS GIBBONS is honest and above the control of the politicians. However, the officers under his control who are in direct contact with the public answer either directly or indirectly to the politicians and crooks." The informant further advised that "the gamblers operating with the various Wards approach the Ward Committeeman and offer to make him a partner in their gambling operation, furnishing to him a partnership share of their profits" in exchange for "the best protection possible from the Ward Committeeman" with great influence over the Ward Magistrate "who is the judicial officer in the lower court." According to the informant "in the event the gambler is arrested his case will be controlled before the Magistrate either by discharge or continuance out of existence."

Philadelphia mobster Dominic Sparagno apparently had a day job, and he "told the Philadelphia Police Department recently that he is employed by the B and J Provisions Company, 1054 Tree Street, Philadelphia Pa." according to a March 1958 FBI report: "this establishment is operated by [redacted] VICTOR CALAMARO, [redacted] of SPARAGNO." An informant corroborated Sparagno's information, and on February 26, 1958 told the FBI "that SPARAGNO is a salesman for this firm, a part of the operations of which consist of catering for parties and dinners." Moreover, this same informant "said that during the 1957 Christmas

Holidays, for example, the firm catered for several affairs given by judges in Philadelphia, and that this business was probably arranged by SPARAGNO in his capacity as salesman."

Michael Maggio's son Peter died in 1992, and the cheese company sold by legitimate heirs nearly two decades ago.

4 GAY MOB ASSOCIATE HEADED BOY TOY CREW

Sam Hoover was a two-term mayor in Pasadena, Texas and a prominent criminal defense attorney but beneath the respectable front lurked a sociopathic thug. The FBI identified Hoover as an associate of Biaggio Angelica who was among the top mobsters in the Lone Star State, and Hoover's principal racket during the 1950s and into the mid-1960s was running an interstate burglary crew comprised largely of teen boys with whom he was sexually involved. The wise guys were fully aware of Hoover's taste for troubled boys — many of whom he kept in living quarters dubbed "the dog house" behind his own residence — and that Hoover was fully immersed in Houston's lively gay nightlife. However, Hoover's sexual proclivities never seemed to undermine his underworld position.

Samuel Wells Hoover was born on December 20, 1908 in Hobart, Oklahoma. In 1943 he enlisted in the U.S. Army, and according to service records saw active duty as an infantryman "in the European-African Middle Eastern Theater from August 28, 1944, to July 20, 1945, and participated in the battle campaigns of Rhineland, Northern France and Central Europe." Hoover "gained two Battle Stars on his campaign ribbon as well as a Good Conduct medal," and was honorably discharged with a sergeant rank on September 27, 1945. Upon returning home he was elected the Pasadena mayor from 1948 to 1951, and attended the South Texas College of Law in Houston from which he graduated in 1951.

Notwithstanding that in 1936 Hoover had multiple arrests on burglary charges in Oklahoma City, the Texas bar licensed Hoover to practice. Hoover became a defense lawyer "representing pimps and prostitutes, con men, thieves, etc.," according to a September 1958 FBI report, and curiously avoided practicing in the federal courts:

> It will be noted during the past week HOOVER has been handling criminal cases in the various courts in Harris County, Houston. It is to be noted HOOVER apparently avoids practice in the Federal courts in Houston, and during the

discussion of another matter with AUSA C. D. COTTINGHAM, SDT, Houston, COTTINGHAM mentioned that HOOVER is known to avoid the Federal courts as there are not any deals to be made in U.S. Courts.

Sam Hoover did not simply represent criminals but ran rackets, and was operating an interstate burglary ring, and his crew of teen boys doubled as his stud stable. A January 1959 FBI memo describes Hoover's Fagin-like predatory recruitment of the juvenile delinquents:

A more realistic view of his role in the affairs of Eastern Texas can be observed in checking the records of numerous youthful offenders who have at one time or another come under his influence. Sam Hoover has followed the practice of spotting likely candidates for his organization who may at the time be in trouble with local authorities, offering his legal services to them, securing their release on bail, and initiating them into his crime organization which consists of a loose-knit group of small gangs who engage in burglaries and robberies at the direction of their attorney. It has also been established that a number of youthful offenders procured in this manner by Sam Hoover have been initiated into practices of perversion to satisfy his lust.

Multiple informants advised that Hoover "always has 'queers' working for him," and crew members in jailhouse interviews admitted that they engaged in "homosexual activity" with Hoover.

A July 1959 FBI report provides that "in regard to the housing of his gang while they are not working, HOOVER possesses a 'dog house' which is a small apartment to the rear of his residence at 500 S. Tatar, Pasadena, where these individuals are housed." The FBI periodically put Sam Hoover under surveillance, and a September 5, 1958 memo states "physical surveillance of the home of HOOVER in Pasadena, Texas, during the past week has developed there is a constant visiting of young men to the offices of HOOVER," and "the young men visiting HOOVER's office usually in the age group of 17 to 20, were not recognized as any known police characters in the Houston area." The Houston Police Department told the FBI on August 15, 1960 that it characterized Hoover's crew as the "kid burglars," and "that during the past few months the number of young 18-19-year-old group burglars apparently employed by HOOVER has been on the increase."

Houston had a well-established gay scene in which Hoover was fully immersed. A July 1959 FBI report states that "information has been obtained that HOOVER is a homosexual and frequently engages in homosexual activities," and a February 29, 1960 memo provides that "surveillances of HOOVER during this past week have resulted in it being ascertained that HOOVER is carrying additional case sometimes referred to as a 'overnight case for queers.'" There were many nightlife establishments in Houston at which Sam Hoover could play. A January 1960 FBI memo states "that the Surf Lounge, The Desert Room, The Pink Elephant and the Stage Door Lounge, Houston, are operating in full swing," and "these are all known hangouts of homosexuals." The same memo also quotes a confidential informant identifying a "Pasadena car dealer as a homosexual" who was "a friend of HOOVER's" and threw "'queer' parties at [his] home." A March 1958 FBI report states that "the socially elite group of homosexuals" attended private parties at Cleve's Steak House on 2834 Holman Road in Houston which otherwise "operates as a legitimate restaurant." An employee from one club told the FBI on October 3, 1960 that "she again saw HOOVER in the company of a 'young kid,'" and "HOOVER was attempting to 'put the make on' the young kid."

Vareece Berry, the former police chief in Pasadena, told the FBI that Hoover was "a well-known homosexual among the hoodlum element in Harris County, TX," and not the least of them was Biaggo Angelica. Angelica made his bones with gambling boss Sam Maceo from Galveston. In 1937 federal prosecutors charged Maceo and Angelica in a sweeping indicting with running southwest distribution for a Mafia-operated narcotics ring which smuggled product from Europe into the New York ports. Maceo was acquitted in 1942 but according to FBI documents Angelica pleaded guilty in 1938, and served several years. Maceo continued his gambling operations, and partnered with Moe Dalitz in opening the Desert Inn in Las Vegas. After Maceo died in 1951 Angelica continued his own gambling and loansharking operations. Angelica owned M&M Music Company out of Galveston which operated jukeboxes, pinball machines, slots and other coin-operated devices, and he owned the Manhattan Lounge at 209 Gray Street in Houston from where he apparently conducted his policy racket. Angelica was a known associate of both Tony Vincent Vallone who allegedly operated "dice games, bookmaking, and other illicit activities" from the Sorrento Restaurant and the Chum Club at 6611 Richmond Road in Houston and Dallas boss Joseph Francis Civello who was among the attending bosses at the infamous 1957 Apalachin meeting.

The FBI uncovered a working relationship between Angelica and Hoover, and the pair often met at Hoover's Pasadena home and office. On December 23, 1958, Angelica bombed a health clinic in High Island, Texas, and upon his arrest police found a certified check on him payable to Hoover. An FBI report states:

> ANGELICA has been reported to be an associate of SAMUEL WELLS HOOVER, a well-known Houston criminal Attorney. At the time ANGELICA was arrested and charged with Arson, he possessed a $2500.00 certified check dated December 15, 1958, payable to SAM HOOVER. HOOVER has advised this was a "business loan" at ten percent interest.

Hoover represented Angelica on the charge, and the local mobster later was convicted of arson.

An informant advised that in October 1959 Hoover visited Dallas "to meet two 'dagos' (Italians) from Kansas City" in connection with his burglary racket. Hoover's burglary ring was not his only racket, and he further was involved with running heroin and marijuana from Mexico and pimping prostitutes and rolling johns in Houston. A July 1959 FBI report in regard to his prostitution activities alleges:

HOOVER has also been reported to have several girls working for him engaged in prostitution. The girls generally operate at the William Penn Hotel and at the Blue Bonnet Motel, Houston. The rate is from $25.00 to $100.00 per trick and approximately $250.00 for all night. The modus operandi followed relative to the prostitution activities is that the girls generally pick up dates at different clubs and lounges around the city of Houston which dates have been directed to the girls by members of HOOVER's gang. Subsequent to being sent to the William Penn Hotel or the Blue Bonnet Motel, the individual desiring a date would be assaulted and rolled after turning a trick. HOOVER's take from the girls has been reported to be 40%.

The rackets generated sufficient income for Hoover to acquire multiple properties and business beyond his legal practice, and according to FBI documents he was "reported to possess an interest in the William Penn Hotel, Houston, several motels, drive-in markets, and furniture company."

Sam Hoover was a tough nut for law enforcement to crack notwithstanding their knowledge of his criminal activities, and he frequently was characterized as "shrewd" or "genius." A September 1959 FBI memo states:

> HOOVER, who is outstanding and almost a genius in the profession of law, has been the subject of many investigations by local and state authorities with the result that HOOVER has to date been successful in evading prosecution. The possibility exists that local and state authorities in their endeavor to prosecute HOOVER have proceeded too hastily, couple with the fact that HOOVER is somewhat of an expert in the loopholes of the law.

One informant told the FBI in June 1959 that Sam Hoover "never discusses illegal business in his office or over his telephone" because "he 'thinks' that his office as well as his phone is 'bugged.'"

In 1958 Hoover was arrested for ordering the murder of underling James Edward Laird whom Hoover thought was flipping although the charge did not stick. The break came for law enforcement in 1964. Texas-cop-turned-crime-writer Larry Watts at his website larrywatts.net vividly describes the gruesome crime which finally brought down Sam Hoover:

> In March of that year, the wealthy owner of a dairy and wholesale grocery supply business, Mair Schepps, his wife, infant child and a family

nurse maid were abducted and tortured as they were held captive in the Schepps River Oaks home. The robbery was set up by Sam Hoover, who never appeared at the crime scene, but gave continuing telephone instructions to the three criminals as they attempted to extract information from the victims about the location of a large sum of cash that Hoover believed Schepps was keeping in the home. The victims were bound and sadistically tortured for three hours. Mrs. Schepps was burned with a butcher knife that was heated on a stove and by cigarettes, wired to an electrical cord and shocked when it was placed on her teeth, breasts, and "private parts." When later arrested, they named Sam Hoover as the mastermind.

Hoover was convicted for his ringleader role but inexplicably released from prison after serving only nineteen years on a sixty-years sentence. The degenerate quickly returned to his old ways, and Watts writes that in 1984 Hoover was returned to prison and died in 1992.

5 FBI AGENTS INVESTIGATED JACK RUBY FOR GAY TIES

President John F. Kennedy was assassinated in Dallas, Texas on November 22, 1963, and two days later on November 24 Jack Ruby killed supposed assassin Lee Harvey Oswald. Rumors long have swirled that Ruby, a local nightclub owner, was at least bisexual if not gay, but doubters say they were just fabrications by New Orleans District Attorney Jim Garrison in order to better link his conspiracy theory about the President's murder to gay businessman and CIA tool Clay Shaw. However, perhaps the Garrison claims that Ruby was gay should not be so quickly dismissed. Just days after Kennedy's assassination the FBI received allegations concerning Ruby's sexual proclivities from Robert Kermit Patterson based on a conversation he overheard at a Dallas gay bar which further mentioned the involvement of "big players" from Chicago and Kansas City.

Patterson's allegations are contained in a November 27, 1963 memo prepared by Special Agent John J. Flanagan. Patterson visited the FBI's Dallas field office on November 27 after hearing a conversation the night before "at one of the 'gay' spots in town, specifically The Villa-Fontana, 1315 Skiles." Patterson claimed he overheard a conversation in which a customer told the bartender – both named Jerry – that "he was a former lover of JACK RUBY," and "that GEORGE SENATOR, roommate of JACK RUBY's at the time of RUBY's arrest, was also a 'gay' person." Moreover, "PATTERSON likewise stated that he heard it mentioned at the Villa-Fontana on November 26, 1963, that LEE HARVEY OSWALD had been seen at the Holiday Bar and also in Gene's Music Bar, both of which PATTERSON described as hangouts for the 'gay' crowd." Gene's Music Bar was at 307 S. Akard which Patterson said "discourages the presence of the female members of the 'gay' set," and the Holiday Bar was at 1212 A Main Street which according to Patterson was a "hangout of the rougher element." The FBI long was aware of the gay scene in Dallas, and in a 1959 report had written that "homosexuals and perverts are known to frequent" the Holiday Bar, 1212-A Main Street, and Music Bar, 307 South Akard.

Perhaps more stunning, Patterson also claimed he overheard from "the conversation between JERRY, the bartender, and JERRY, the customer, . . . something to the effect that five 'big people' were involved in the assassination of President JOHN F. KENNEDY," and "to the best of his recollection, the five 'big people' were described as being one from Dallas, two from Chicago and two from Kansas City." Patterson "stressed that he did not overhear the full conversation concerning this matter and was merely trying to repeat that portion which he had heard," and "he said he did not understand the full significance of it."

A few days later on November 27, 1963 FBI agents asked Chicago Outfit mobster Jimmy "the Monk" Allegretti and his suspected gay bar front Nate Zuckerman what they knew about Jack Ruby. Allegretti was the Rush Street crew boss who ran the vice rackets – gay bars, strip clubs, whore houses, gambling dens – from the mid-1940s to the mid-1960s on the Near North Side for Chicago Outfit underboss Ross Prio, and in the FBI interview he denied knowing Ruby although with typical wise guy attitude "indicated that he was not sure whether he would be willing to discuss him if he would have any information concerning this man."

An FBI memo dated December 17, 1963 by Special Agent August C. Kempff summarizes this interview with Allegretti as follows:

On November 29, 1963, JAMES ALLEGRETTI was contacted in Room 1177 of Wesley Memorial Hospital by SAs AUGUST C. KEMPFF and [name redacted]. ALLEGRETTI was contacted for the purpose of inquiring as to any knowledge he may have had concerning JACK LEON RUBY and RUBY's previous residence in the Chicago area. On entering Room 1177 ALLEGRETTI was observed in the company of four male persons three of whom were unidentified and the other was [name redacted] is a lieutenant of ALLEGRETTI's and formerly operated the lounge in the Devonshire Hotel and has alleged to be a collector and payoff man for ALLEGRETTI's gambling activities. One of the unknown persons at the time of the Agents entry to the room was observed counting out money to ALLEGRETTI from a sizable roll of bills. As the Agents entered the room and were recognized by ALLEGRETTI this man discontinued counting money and both ALLEGRETTI and the unknown individual put the money they were handling out of view. ALLEGRETTI stated that he did not know JACK RUBY and indicated that he was not sure whether he would be willing to discuss him if he would have any information concerning this man.

According to this same report the FBI also suspected gay bar operator Nate Zuckerman as an Allegretti associate, and interviewed either him or an employee – the name is redacted – at the Front Page Lounge at Rush and Grand Streets who similarly disclaimed knowing Ruby:

<u>NATE ZUCKERMAN</u>

[Name redacted] was characterized by [informant] as an employee of JIMMY ALLEGRETTI who has been an associate of his over many years. [Name redacted] was said to be the bartender in the downstairs "gay" bar of the Front Page Lounge, located at Rush and Grand Streets, Chicago. [Name redacted] was contacted concerning any knowledge he may have concerning JACK LEON RUBY and stated he did not know RUBY. [Name redacted] stated that although he would ordinarily not furnish any information to the Federal Bureau of Investigation in the case of JACK RUBY he would be willing to help if he were able.

Two years earlier, an FBI informant alleged that

he saw Allegretti at a nightclub with the owner of Jay Potato Chips who supposedly was grousing over the Kennedy Administration crackdown against the mob. A December 19, 1961 memo by Special Agent Edward J. Nehls states the following:

> [Informant] advised in August, 1961 that he observed JAMES ALLEGRETTI at the Shh club in company with a Mr. Jay, owner of Jay Potato Chips. Mr. Jay appeared to be very well acquainted with ALLEGRETTI and was voicing around that the Kennedy Administration is unduly harassing the so-called hoodlums.

The then-owner of Jay Potato Chips actually was Leonard Japp, Sr. – the brand previously was Japp's Potato Chips – who allegedly got his start by delivering nuts and pretzels to Al Capone's speakeasies in 1927, and it is unclear whether the informant was referring to Mr. Japp.

The FBI interview with Allegretti confirms that it was interested in a possible mob connection to the Kennedy assassination from the very beginning. Indeed, the feds perhaps were right about their instincts. The evidence compiled over the years suggests that in the mid-1940s Ruby did work in Chicago for a seedy joint or two which may have been associated with Allegretti according to some investigators.

6 GERMANO CRIME FAMILY OPERATED ALBANY GAY BARS

The Germano brothers were big players in the Albany underworld from the 1920s into the early 1960s, and they were tied to at least two gay bars. These Germano establishments were among many bars serving gays and lesbians during the 1950s and 1960s in the New York capital city.

The five brothers – James, Charles, William, Joseph and Salvatore or Sammy – used the alias King as their surname, and were headed by Willie or "the Yellow King" whose rackets included bootlegging, dope peddling and bookmaking. Willie Germano infamously got away with the 1922 murder of Patsy Farina in a turf dispute involving heroin sales. The Germano brothers were widely respected among Albany hoodlums. Jimmy Germano was gunned down on February 14, 1931 by Joseph La Tassa, the son of Black Hand boss Angelo La Tassa, and his funeral attracted a "huge crowd" of 3,000 people including "several of Albany's 'big shots' in underworld circles" according to a front page story in the *Times Union.*

The Germano brothers were protected by Dan O'Donnell who ran the Albany County Democratic organization for more than fifty years until his 1977 death. Willie Germano had a no-show front job with the water department, and helped run the Democrat machine's vote-buying schemes — $5 a vote — at election times. O'Donnell was not just a machine boss but also the underworld head, and he consolidated illegal gambling. All bookmakers in the capital city were on a 50-50 basis with O'Donnell associates Hank Corscadden and Dan Durando, and further were required to make "annual political contributions" to the Democrat boss according to multiple FBI confidential informants. The intermediary between the gambling underworld and the O'Donnell machine who both gave the okay for illicit operations and collected the tribute payments was identified in FBI documents as Leo C. Quinn who was the executive secretary of the Albany County Democratic organization and superintendent of the Bureau of Tax Delinquencies. As one informant summed it up to the FBI in 1958: "operation of bookmaking in Albany is political."

The main shylock for the Albany bookmakers was Nate Weinstein according to an FBI memo:

Confidential Informant Albany T-20, previously mentioned, on November 14, 1958, mentioned that NATE WEINSTEIN, liquor dealer who had an establishment at Maiden Lane and Broadway, Albany, and who recently died, was a "shylock" for bookmakers of Albany, charging them ten percent. The informant said that no one had replaced WEINSTEIN in this capacity since his death and he did not know of anyone likely to as no one had the cash or the contacts.

Weinstein operated Super Wine and Liquor at 496 Broadway, and was controlled by New York City mobsters. In October 1956 Carmine Galente was picked up on a speeding ticket near Binghamton after a mob meeting with Joseph Barbara at his Apalachin farm, and Weinstein had reached out to Vincent Macri, a shadowy fixer in the state capital, in an unsuccessful attempt to dismiss the charge against the Bonanno boss. A year later Weinstein suffered a heart attack which left him in a vegetative state, and Stephen Scepkowski, a lackey from the Albany office of Carmine DeSapio, immediately took over the management of his liquor store. DeSapio was the Tammany Hall boss from New York City, and even at that time was widely-known as nothing more than a mob tool running interference for and providing protection to Frank Costello and other Genovese hoodlums.

King's Cafe at 68 Madison Avenue opened in 1939 when the property was purchased by Willie's wife Antoinette Germano and her mother Elizabeth Belmonte. The two-story brick building was "one of the oldest business properties in the South End" which "has been completely remodeled in modernistic style" according to an October 27, 1939 *Times Union* article:

> The entire first floor is now occupied by King's Cafe. The interior has been rearranged into two large main rooms with the main bar occupying the front room and the oyster and clam bar located in the rear room and adjoining the dance floor. The New York style of cafe has been incorporated as much as possible in the arrangement, even to the extent of installation of tables formerly used in Jim Braddock's cafe in New York City.

Over the years it was targeted multiple times by State Liquor Authority inspectors for various infractions. It is unclear at what point it attracted gay patrons but in 1953 was cited for, among other things, permitting "homosexuals to loiter" according to an August 25, 1954 article from the *Times Union*:

Samuel J. Germano, manager of King's Cafe, 68 Madison Ave., yesterday denied at a State Liquor Authority hearing that he tried to bribe an SLA investigator with money last fall. Germano contended that the only thing he offered Milton E. Andre, the investigator, was a cigar. Three other SLA charges were denied by Germano's brother, Charles, who holds the license for King's. They are employment of a convicted felon, permitting disorderly altercation on the premises and permitting homosexuals to loiter.

King's Cafe lost its license for a year due to the multiple violations. Willie died in 1960, and King's Cafe subsequently was closed by the Liquor Authority in May 1963 after it was cited this time for "permitting unescorted women to meet with unescorted men for immoral purposes."

Another premise which catered to gay patrons was Belmonte's Restaurant at 38 North Clark Street operated by Pastsy Belmonte who was the brother of Willie's wife Antoinette. Belmonte's Restaurant was shut down by the Liquor Authority in November 1963 for permitting "the licensed premises to become disorderly in that homosexuals, degenerates and undesirables were permitted to congregate on the licensed premises."

Numerous other gay bars in Albany were targeted for enforcement action by the Liquor Authority during the 1950s and 1960s including Yock's Restaurant at 90 ½ Hudson Avenue ("permitting homosexuals and lesbians to loiter for immoral purposes" per 03/27/54 *Knickerbocker News*); Clancy's Grill at 529 Broadway ("men who swung their hips, spoke in high-pitched voices and called each other by such names as Freda, Gigi and Queenie" per 10/03/59 *Knickerbocker News*); The Point at 25-27 Daniel Street ("while the juke box blared, girls with crew-cuts and boys with flopping hands were dancing in the middle of the room" per 03/24/61 *Knickerbocker News*); Market Square Bar at 9 Market Street ("allowing homosexuals and degenerates to gather and immoral acts committed in bar" per 05/25/61 *Times Union*); Circular Tap Room at 456 Broadway ("permitted homosexuals, degenerates and other persons to remain on the licensed premises" per 09/30/61 *Times Record*); Fort Orange Grill at 352 Broadway ("allowing homosexuals, degenerates and undesirable characters to loiter" per 10/06/61 *Times Union*); Gilmer's at 60 Green Street ("a regular resort by homosexuals" where "male patrons when they walked, swayed their hips, wore tight-fitting clothing, spoke in high-pitched voices and waved their hands in the air with limp wrists" per 12/21/63 *Knickerbocker News*); and Hanley's Restaurant & Grill at 107 Clinton Avenue ("several females with short haircuts and no makeup dressed in mannish attire and men in tight-fitting clothes, dirty blond hair and high-pitched voices" per 02/10/65 *Knickerbocker News*).

Many of these establishments were located in lower downtown inner Albany known as the South End or "the Gut" which was a working class ethnic enclave where Democratic boss Dan O'Donnell grew up. The licensees of these establishments were an odd-ball assortment including shady Italians, ex-cops and the politically connected, and some places had undisclosed interests held by convicted felons. For example, Frank Berghela had an undisclosed interest in The Point, and his rap sheet went back to 1927 when he was eighteen years old and a member of the so-called "boy bandit" crew which was responsible for 15 robberies. Clancy's Grill was run by Louis J. Vita, a former Albany police officer, and he testified at the SLA hearing that he could not determine if someone were "a deviate or not" pointedly adding "I don't ask people if they're homosexuals — I would have my head bashed in." The operator of Gilmer's was Marion Gilmer, one of the few black bar owners at that time, and his wife Shirley Gilmer was appointed to the Citizens'

Advisory Committee for Urban Renewal by O'Donnell lapdog Mayor Erastus Corning 2nd although she resigned after her husband's gay bar bust.

The Albany police rarely raided the vice district in the Gut which in addition to queer joints also had bars for B-girls, prostitutes, gamblers and hoodlums. One informant advised the FBI according to a 1958 report that many cops were on the take: "At Albany, according to Confidential Informant Albany T-19, who has furnished reliable information in the past, and based on talk to the informant of madams and prostitutes, practically every detective and uniformed man on the night squad of the Albany Police Department 'take' from the houses of prostitution." Enforcement action pretty much was left to the Liquor Authority including a 1961 operation in which Governor Rockefeller ordered an SLA team from New York City to target dozens of seedy joints in the Gut just to annoy Dan O'Connell and his Democrat hacks.

Many of the targeted establishments in the 1961 operation "had been financed through a syndicate-type operation" according to a May 25, 1961 article from the *Times Union*. The paper did not identify the financing source but in 1959 an FBI informant advised that three jukebox vendors – Harmonies at

113 South Pearl, Melodies, Inc. at 11 North Pearl and another concern – were the principal loan sources for Albany watering holes:

On May 20, 1959, Confidential Informant Albany T-21 advised SA [redacted] that shylocking activities in Albany are carried out on a large basis by three people controlling the juke boxes installed at various taverns and restaurants in Albany. He identified these people as [redacted] of Harmony Studio located at Van Zandt and Pearl Street over Jean's Bar and who is a partner along with [redacted] with offices at 91 State Street; first name unrecalled [redacted] of Melody Juke Box, 11 North Pearl Street; and [redacted] who is just starting in the business. He stated that [redacted] and [redacted] control the straight talk box-type wherein a direct connection is made with a live operator who then plays wired music as requested. He stated that [redacted] obliges his clients to take his box on a three to four year contract basis, gets a 50% split on the juke box proceeds and a large interest rate on loans which he makes to the owners. He advised that all three of these individuals will loan any restaurant or tavern owner money amounting from $5,000.00 to $10,000.00 if they will install their particular type of juke box. He said that [redacted] charges the most exorbitant rate of interest and that [redacted] money is obtained from the [redacted].

Of course, periodic clampdowns had little lasting impact on the neighborhood vice, and in response to the 1961 sweep "many of the most flagrant violators told a team of reporters" that "this will all pass over" and "we'll be back" according to the May 25 report from the *Times Union*. Indeed, as the same article aptly pointed out: "in the past the bar owners have merely gone underground, picked up an honest face for a front and gone back in business with the man with the honest face putting his name on the license."

7 1962 CLAMPDOWN ON ROCHESTER GAY BARS

In 1962 the State Liquor Authority cancelled the licenses of three gay bars in Rochester, New York – Patsy's Grill licensed to Pasquale and Katherine Lippa at 278 Allen Street, Dick's Tavern licensed to Dominic Gruttadauria at 63 State Street and Martin's Restaurant licensed to Harry Martin at 12 Front Street – according to articles from the *Democrat & Chronicle*.

The three establishments previously had been identified in FBI memos. In a March 17, 1958 memo the FBI reported "the following places are gathering spots for homosexuals in Rochester": Martin's Tavern, 12 Front Street; Nite Cap Tavern, 393 Court Street; Dick's Tavern, 14 Front Street; Peg and Larry's Tavern, 19 Front Street; and RDGA, Franklin Square. Four years later an FBI memo identified "homosexual and lesbian hangouts" which further included Patsy's Grill at 278 Allen Street. Several men's rooms and public parks also were listed for gay hookups in the 1962 memo: Rochester Public Library Men's Room, 115 South Avenue; Baptist Temple Building Men's Room, 14 Franklin Street; Waldorf Cafeteria, Men's Room and Restaurant, 10 East Main Street; Sibley's Department Store (men's room in basement), 228 East Main Street; Edward's Department Store Men's Room, 144 East Main Street; Greyhound Bus Depot Men's Room, 320 Andrews Street; Blue Valley Bus Terminal Men's Room, 83 South Avenue; River Boulevard along the railroad tracks; Broad and Court Street Bridges; and Maplewood Park.

The charges against Patsy's, Martin's and Dick's were announced in January 1962 following a year-long investigation in which "the SLA sent its agents in inconspicuous dress into the bars as a result of public complaints," and "after observing conditions, the investigators did not reveal themselves but wrote reports to the SLA." The reports accused the establishments of "permitting 'open and notorious' homosexual activity without action to curb or halt the practices." Within months the licenses for all three were quickly cancelled after their respective SLA hearings.

Dr. G Harold Warnock, the deputy county health director in Monroe County responsible for tracking venereal disease, was happy to see the Liquor Authority shut down the gay bars. He told the *Democrat & Chronicle* that "there were other areas in the city 'just about as bad' as Front Street," and "he branded homosexual activity as a contributory cause of spreading infection but not the chief cause."

The clampdown on the gay bars should be of little surprise given the homophobia that still persisted into the 1960s but Rochester seemed unusually stubborn in clinging to its anachronistic prejudices. In 1964 the *Democrat & Chronicle* ran a four-part series by Pat Ziska called "The Outcasts" in an ugly campaign against the "national movement . . . to relax the laws against homosexuals." The first article from March 15 explored "the extent of the community's involvement in this growing problem," and the Rochester Police Bureau provided the paper with a list of nearly 300 known homosexuals it was tracking. The list was compiled by policewoman Joan V. Mathers who headed the Morals Squad, and it "showed that the known deviates range in age from the mid-sixties to under 13":

She [Mathers] produced pictures of two attractive girls, one a blonde, the other a brunette. Then she displayed a picture of two

21-year-old youths. The two "girls" in the photos were really the two boys dressed in feminine attire complete with expensive wigs. They had been stopped recently by police for a traffic violation and their true identity was discovered when the arresting officer looked at the driver's license. "We now have their names, pictures and other vital information on file," policewoman Mather said, "and we'll keep track of them."

According to the March 15 article the Rochester Police Bureau "makes an effort to answer complaints and suppress solicitation in places like taverns, downtown bridges, parks and lavatories in public buildings." Indeed, from 1958 through 1963 "there were 119 arrests for sodomy, many involving homosexuals," and "besides these charges, hundreds of arrests have been made for loitering, intoxication, disorderly conduct, vagrancy and other charges in which the principals are homosexuals."

The following day on March 16 the *Democrat & Chronicle* ran its second article in "The Outcasts" series which provided a voyeuristic look into the gay "cult" including a Friday night visit to one of the downtown bars which was crowded "with more than 100 persons" and "the floor was jammed with 12 pairs of dancers, mostly men":

A young man named Jimmy was the most active of the dancers and kept up a near marathon, changing partners frequently. Jimmy wasn't difficult to follow with the eyes. Like most of the younger men, he wore tight fitting khaki trousers. But his shirt was red and white peppermint striped. He received many compliments on the shirt, described as a "blouse" by some of the habitués.

In further educating readers about the gay world the March 16 article reported that "Halloween is the national homosexual holiday," and "it is on this day that many of them dress in female garb or 'drag' and attend parties, usually in private homes or buildings." The Rochester Police Bureau learned about the Halloween phenomenon in the gay community by attending a "seminar on homosexuality" provided by the FBI "for local police bureaus and departments," and told the *Democrat & Chronicle* that its undercover vice officers had infiltrated "such parties."

The third article from March 17 interviewed a 24-year-old married gay man with four children who "admitted that he married only to have a family and also to cloak himself in respectability," and he told the *Democrat & Chronicle*: "I seek out male companions from one to three times a week. It varies. When I go out, my wife thinks I'm working. I have that kind of job." The married man attended private parties or gay bars but said he loathed the homosexuals who publicly cruised "Broad Street or Court Street bridges or in Maplewood Park": "I know some who are on the prowl. They should be put behind bars. * * * If they bother people, I say put them away. They aren't our kind. They're out for money. Otherwise they'd join our group."

The concluding March 18 article in the four-part Outcasts series focused on psychiatric problems, and closed with a warning by policewoman Joan Mathers from the Morals Squad:

> "Parents should be made aware of the problems and should warn their children against homosexuals and other types of molesters. Anyone who has read The Democrat and Chronicle series should now be aware of the danger of this unhappy and undesirable way of life. I would say the next step is up to parents."

The *Democrat & Chronicle* conveniently timed its four-part series just as state legislators in Albany were proposing to reform the sodomy laws, and Rochester Police Chief William M. Lombard and Monroe County Sheriff Albert W. Skinner publicly objected to any changes in a March 19 article:

> "As a law enforcement agent I would be against any change to reduce the law," said Lombard. "It

would give the true criminal homosexual another out and create one more defense for such persons. It would then be difficult to establish 'consent' and thus be tougher to prosecute criminally active homosexuals." Skinner said he, too, was against any mitigation of the law for the same reasons. "It certainly wouldn't help," he explained, "we're having trouble enough with them now."

In response to the series the *Democrat & Chronicle* received many letters from readers which "described the bitterness and loneliness of their outcast experience," and the paper reprinted one from "an older homosexual" on the "very lonely life": "As I sit at the gay bar night after night, I can't help wondering to myself what will happen to these (younger) boys 20 years from now. Today they think it is all a big blast, but believe me it isn't." The letter was anonymously signed "Just another outcast."

8 BUFFALO MOVIE THEATER WAS GAY CRUISING GROUND

The Little Hippodrome – known locally as the Little Hip – opened in 1903 at 263 Main Street as the first motion picture theater in Buffalo, New York, and from the late 1940s through the mid-1950s was popular among gay men as a cruising ground. During this period dozens of men were arrested by the Buffalo Police Vice Squad headed by Lieutenant Albert F. Saxer, and for those convicted prison time at the notorious Attica state prison was not uncommon according to multiple *Buffalo Evening News* reports from the period.

For example, on October 5, 1948 57-year-old Ahmed Hassen and his sex partner 31-year-old Charles Savage were arrested in the basement of the Little Hippodrome. The pair quickly pleaded guilty to second-degree assault charges, and on December

16 both were given prison time. Hassen received 2 ½ to 5 years in Attica, and County Judge Carlton Fisher justified the lengthy term because he was convicted of a morals charge in 1937, and maybe this time would learn his lesson. The sentencing judge moralized:

> "I think I have a solution. We must protect society. It is true perhaps that this man should be in a medical institution, but there are none for such persons under conviction. Prison may teach him to restrain any unnatural urge which may come upon him in the future."

Hassen's defense lawyer Harry J. Lipsitz had urged clemency from the judge by bringing into court a copy of the Kinsey report but Judge Fisher dismissed it. And Savage – the younger man was so frightened at the time of his arrest gave cops a false name – was sentenced to just a year in the county prison since he had no prior record.

On December 16, 1948 Judge Fisher sentenced 77-year-old John Sperry to a 2 ½ to 5 year term at Attica on a second-degree assault conviction following his arrest with another man at the Little Hippodrome but suspended it because Sperry had no prior record and had a 74-year-old wife. Not all the arrests involved sex with consenting adults. On December 17, 1948 24-year-old Richard Burger was busted at the Little Hippodrome, and he pleaded guilty to a morals charge involving a 14-year-old boy. Burger received prison time but since the conviction was for a misdemeanor the sentence was less than a year.

Other convictions for gay cruising at the Little Hippodrome during the 1948-1949 sweep by the vice squad according to reports from the *Buffalo Evening News* included the following: 32-year-old Russell Gugino was arrested on October 30, 1948, convicted of third-degree assault, and given a suspended one-year sentence; and 32-year-old Robert Smith was arrested on November 24, 1948, convicted of second-degree assault, and given a suspended sentence of 2 ½ to 5 years at Attica. The men additionally were fined and placed on probation, and a subsequent arrest would result in probation revocation and immediate remand to serve the sentence. For example, 20-year-old Chariot Johnson was arrested on November 20, 1948 at the Little Hippodrome, and given a suspended one-year sentence and three-years' probation on a morals conviction; however, when he was arrested on the same charge in April 1949 in the Twentieth Century Theater at 511 Main Street, City Judge Jacob Latona imposed the one-year sentence from the earlier conviction.

Gay men used the Little Hippodrome for public sex at least well into the 1950s. On January 22, 1952, Chief City Judge John W. Ryan Jr. sentenced John Davis to six months behind bars for "offering to commit an indecent act" in an undercover sting by Lieutenant Saxer's vice squad. On November 10, 1953 Judge Ryan sentenced Clarence Hamler to a six-month prison term following his conviction from an October 19 undercover sting, and the sentencing judge expressly stated the hard time was "for the good of the community." Hamler had a record going back to 1911 involving 91 previous arrests including a narcotics conviction. Among Hamler's nine aliases over the years was "Lady Irene." And on February 29, 1956 24-year-old Edward Gallagher got a six-month prison term on a morals conviction from a February 13 incident at the theater.

Sometimes the men arrested on morals charges at the Little Hippodrome were allowed to plead guilty to lesser charges out of rare moments of purported compassion from sentencing judges. For example, 72-year-old Salvatore Mattina was arrested on April 12, 1955 "on a charge of loitering to commit an immoral act" but "was allowed to plead guilty to public intoxication," and the judge accepted the reduced plea and gave a suspended six-month sentence due to his old age.

The Little Hippodrome closed on November 9, 1962 and demolished in 1963 but there were other venues for gay men to meet. A March 17, 1958 FBI memo reported "the following are the bars frequented by homosexuals and lesbians" based on intelligence from the then-head of the Vice & Liquor Squad of the Buffalo Police Department: Carousel Bar & Grill, 457 Ellicott Street; Johnny's 68 Club, 68 Genesee Street; The Club Oasis, 60 Genesee Street; The Kitty Kat, 97 Genesee Street; The Imperial Bar, 529 Washington Street; Dugan's Bar and Grill, 29 North Division Street; Bingo's Bar, 90 East Eagle Street; The 5 O'clock Club, 285 Delaware Avenue; The Chesterfield Club, 42 East Eagle Street; and The Mardi Gras, 52 East Eagle Street. An October 31, 1958 report included the additional places on the FBI's gay bar list: Fundy's, 531 Washington Street; Gaiety Bar, 520 Washington Street; The Tudor Arms Motel Bar, Franklin and Tupper Streets; 492 Club, 492 Pearl Street; and Stage Door, 414 Pearl Street. A September 9, 1959 report added the following: Alibi Bar, 18 Chippewa Street; Wonderbar, 392 Pearl Street; Maroon Grill, 382 Pearl Street; and Silver Dollar, 44 West Chippewa Street. The 5 O'clock Club at 285 Delaware Avenue was operated by Julius Timineri, and in 1959 the State Liquor Authority suspended his license 40 days for operating a disorderly premise.

In addition to patronage by the locals apparently "these places are also visited by the Canadian element who come here on holidays and weekends" according to the October 31, 1958 report, and a police source advised the FBI that homosexual busts never were made in the premises but outside: "[N]o arrest on the premises of any of these listed places. He stated that contact has been made in a number of them and arrests following later after the homosexual had taken the police officer to a room or vacant lot." In 1961 the Buffalo police arrested 295 "male sex deviates" according to a March 1962 FBI report.

A 1958 memo identified Club Coco at 829 Michigan Avenue as "frequented by Negro pimps, prostitutes, homosexuals, Lesbians and sadists." The premise reportedly was owned by brothers Irving and Louis Weinstein, and apparently they had the place bugged to monitor customer conversations:

> On February 26, 1958, in connection with a White Slave Traffic Act investigation, [redacted] admitted that numerous Negro prostitutes, who are also lesbian, are now frequenting this club and, in fact, several of them are employed as hostesses, including [redacted] and [redacted]. Information has been received from informants .

. . that both colored and white prostitutes are soliciting tricks at the bar at the Club Coco. It should also be noted that [redacted] has admitted that certain parts of the club are wired including the men's room, the ladies' room, the kitchen and two sections of the bar. The [redacted] can listen in on an intercommunication system in their office to conversations engaged in by patrons of this club if they so desire.

Lesbian prostitutes apparently were making their home at the Hotel Delmar at 201 West Huron Street in Buffalo according to a September 9, 1959 report: "[Redacted] at the Hotel Delmar, has furnished information that white and colored lesbians are residing at the Delmar Hotel," and "after making contact at a local bar, tavern or night club can bring their dates back to the hotel to fill them." The Delmar was owned and operated by Louis La Voie, and he was "known to the Vice and Liquor Squad inasmuch as he formerly operated the LaVoie Hotel and Massage Parlor on East Mohawk Street, Buffalo, a number of years ago, which place was padlocked for allowing prostitution and homosexual acts to transpire."

9 GAY BAR HOPPING ACROSS THE USA

In the late 1950s and early 1960s the FBI conducted surveys of crime conditions across the United States, and part of its assessment included the identification of bars or "notorious places of amusement" where the criminal element, juvenile delinquents, narcotics users, sex deviates and other marginalized people congregated. Most information was provided to the FBI from local law enforcement, and revealed that in the pre-Stonewall era the gay subculture was pervasive throughout the country including in surprising places.

In California the FBI files reflect gay action from San Diego to Los Angeles to San Francisco. In San Diego men were cruising in Balboa Park, and the police department revealed to the FBI its entrapment program according to a 1959 report:

On March 25, 1959, Sergeant [redacted] in

charge of San Diego Police Department Sex Crime Detail, advised that during the past year, in an effort to combat the increased homosexual offenses in San Diego, a new program has been utilized. Records reflected that the most aggravated spot for sex perverts was Balboa Park.

Apparently the entrapment program centered around "a young patrol officer in plain clothes" who was "selected for his appearance and cordiality," and the report further provides:

He is instructed to maintain a friendly attitude and to greet everyone he meets while strolling through the park with a nod and a smile. When a suspect (male) exhibits a friendly attitude toward the officer, the officer strolls toward a secluded area in the park. If the suspect follows, the officer leads him into a conversation concerning the trees, the weather, etc. If the suspect indicates an apparent interest in the officer the officer quotes some given phrase, such as "What do you like?" It has been found that the suspect, if a homosexual, generally interprets this phrase as a "come on" as to the type of sex deviation he is interested in. The suspect is then arrested if he makes an overt act toward or on the officer.

The most disturbing revelation in this report is that

the San Diego Police Department was suborning perjury by instructing its undercover officer to lie under oath by testifying at trial he was not using the phrase "what do you like" as a "come on" to target the homosexual: "If the officer testifies in court, for instance, if the suspect pleads not guilty, the officer testifies that in using the phrase 'what do you like?' he was referring to a sport, such as tennis, golf, lawn bowling, etc."

The entrapment program was launched in February 1958, and was considered a resounding success by San Diego's sex police: "Sergeant [redacted] and other officers have advised that this operation has considerably reduced the number of sex pervert complaints received by the department, and thereby identified a number of these individuals who might perpetrate more serious crimes if the opportunity were available." The arrested homosexuals were identified as follows:

> Since the inception of this procedure approximately 100 arrests have been made. The suspect is generally charged with vagrancy — lewd and dissolute, indecent exposure and/or loitering. All classes of persons have been arrested, including school teachers, ministers, beauty operators, aircraft employees, sales clerks, the credit manager of a large store, a rancher,

laborers, a police sergeant, El Cajon Police Department, and recently a U.S. Internal Revenue Agent. The Police Sergeant and Internal Revenue Agent were referred to their respective supervisor officers. In the case of the Police Sergeant, he was permitted to resign.

Many gay bars existed in San Francisco, and an FBI September 1959 report claims "all of the following establishments in the San Francisco area are known hangouts of homosexuals and sex deviates and are patronized exclusively by these individuals": Paper Doll, 524 Union Street; 57 Club, 57 Powell Street; Black Cat, 710 Montgomery Street; Handlebar, 1438 California Street; Spur Club, 126 Turk Street; Hideaway, 438 Eddy Street; Nob Hill, 2223 Polk Street; Fez, 162 Turk Street; 585 Club, 585 Post Street; Nellie's, 789 Howard Street; Roland's, 3309 Fillmore Street; Gordon's, 840 Sansome Street; Kelly's, 800 Fulton Street; Who Cares, 782 Haight Street; Opus One, 734-38 Montgomery Street; Don's, 1192 Pine Street; Cinema, 301 Turk Street; Copper Lantern, 1335 Grant Street; Dolan's, 406 Stockton Street; Crossroads, 109 Steuart Street; Castaways, 90 Market Street; The Fan, 220 Turk Street; Silver Dollar, 64 Eddy Street; Aloha, 145 Eddy Street; Ensign, 1 Market Street; Lariat, 138 Mason Street; Caprice

Room, 3166 Buchanan Street; New Rainbow, 2191 Union Street; Denny Barrell House, 88 Embarcadero; Gene's, 99 Broadway Street; Flamingo, Sausalito, California; Bridgewood, Sausalito, California; and Traveler's Inn, 901 Tamalpais, San Rafael, California.

The FBI further identified – but redacted her name – "a well-known Lesbian who operates a hangout for deviates in San Francisco," and the lesbian also was a madam. Among those she was pimping out to johns for $100 was a call girl who nearly fifteen years earlier was an actress getting banged by Los Angeles mobster Mickey Cohen and *Scarface* actor George Raft. Apparently the one-time mob moll whose name also is redacted in the FBI memo "first hit the headlines in 1945 as an 18-year-old Hollywood starlet whose sordid affair with movie actor George Raft came to a sudden close when she sought legal means of recovering furs, jewelry and expensive gifts which Raft had taken back from her after tiring of her."

Los Angeles always has been a gay Mecca which the FBI aptly noted in a 1958 memo which states "regarding sexual deviates, while no statistics are available, there can be little doubt that Los Angeles is home to as many, or probably more, of this class than are to be found in any other city in the country." Indeed, the FBI cited that "the 'queer tank' at the Los Angeles County Jail is usually over-populated, despite its generous size."

The same report further provides that "occasionally, one of the more prominent of such people gets arrested, such as the case of JOHN CABELL (BUNNY) BRECKINRIDGE, 57-year-old socialite heir to the Comstock Lode fortune and resident of San Francisco" and "a great grandson of the pre-Civil War Vice President of the United States." According to the FBI "BRECKINRIDGE was arrested by Los Angeles Police Department officers August 6, 1958, as he checked into the Beverly Hilton Hotel just inside the City Limits of Beverly Hills," and "accused of committing felony sex offenses against two brothers, ages 11 and 13 years, from Pebble Beach, California." The FBI described "Bunny" as a "millionaire who wears mascara and perfume," and "several years ago he announced he intended to undergo an operation, transforming him into a woman."

The crime to which Breckinridge confessed was quite disturbing. The two boys had been entrusted into his care by "a Pebble Beach society matron, while she went to Lake Tahoe for a vacation," and after he had his way with them Breckinridge passed the poor things off to his friends. The FBI report states the following:

BRECKINRIDGE brought the boys to Los Angeles and when he returned to Northern California, told the mother he had left her sons with a friend in Hollywood. The mother filed a missing person's report, which was forwarded to the Los Angeles police. They located the children at the apartment of [name redacted] of Hollywood. He was arrested, as was [name redacted] also of Hollywood, who like [name reacted] was booked on the charge of felony crime against children. [Name redacted] admitted accompanying BRECKINRIDGE and the two boys from Carmel to Las Vegas, where they spent four days in July before proceeding to Hollywood.

The FBI also noted a Los Angeles vice raid in 1958 during which one prostitute "was discovered to be not as thoroughly female as the others":

In spite of the sordidness, police sometimes get a chuckle incidental to handling these girls. For example, on July 2 a raiding party of Metropolitan Division officers rounded up a sizeable group of Negro prostitutes soliciting on a street. The girls were all booked at the female section of the jail and were then disrobed for the usual bath. At this point, one was discovered to be not as thoroughly female as the others. Questioned about "her" life as a prostitute, this masquerader explained that he would apologize to his "tricks," offering them only unnatural sex activity due to a normal female phenomenon.

Among the bars in Los Angeles which the FBI identified as "notorious places . . . because of the type of clientele they cater to" were the following: The Rag Doll, 11702 Victory Boulevard, North Hollywood; The Hen House, 7847 Van Nuys Boulevard, Van Nuys; The Palomino, 6907 Lankershim Boulevard, North Hollywood; The Greenwich Village, 11644 Ventura Boulevard, Sherman Oaks (reportedly a place frequented by lesbians); Sir Sico, 8351 San Fernando Road, Sun Valley (run, and possibly owned by FRANK SICA); Rocky's Bar, 10909 Burbank Boulevard, North Hollywood; Herbie's Tavern, 7719 Sam Fernando Road, Sun Valley; and The Play Pen Bar, 11685 Ventura Boulevard, Studio City.

In 1958 the Santa Monica police department was busy shutting down gay bars according to the FBI report: "with a continuing drive by Santa Monica Police Department on homosexuals who congregate in the beach area of Santa Monica - Ocean Park, the Tropic Village, a notorious hangout for homosexuals, has closed and activities at the

Captain's Inn seriously curtailed to such an extent, it is also expected to close." Further down the coast in Long Beach the Grass Shack Drive-In at 1911 East Pacific Coast Highway was "frequented by male 'queers,'" and the Pizza House at 351 East Broadway was patronized by "juvenile male 'queers' and young sailors."

In Hawaii the civilians were corrupting servicemen according to FBI files addressing the "homosexual situation." A March 1, 1962 memo identifies "the number of cases involving service personnel relations with homosexuals in the Waikiki area." For example, the Marine Corps Air Station, Kaneohe, reported that "17 station personnel within the previous several month period had been investigated and admitted homosexual activities, both passive and active, with males encountered in the Waikiki area." The Hawaii Armed Services Police conducted an investigation of the service personnel involved, and "compiled a list of 176 males in the Waikiki area, not service personnel, who have been identified as homosexuals." Apparently they were a sneaky lot, and "the principal homosexuals frequently move their residences in the Waikiki area to escape police detection."

The "principal hangouts for homosexuals in the Honolulu area were reported as follows": Swiss

Chalet, Kailua, Oahu; The Clouds and Little Dipper both at 124 Kapahulu Avenue, Waikiki; Wagon Wheel Restaurant, 27 Kalakaua Avenue, Waikiki; and Le Coq D'or, 1900 Kalakaua Avenue, Waikiki. The Little Dipper was a bar "located on the street floor of the Park Surf hotel, Waikiki, while The Clouds is a restaurant bar located on the second floor." The Little Dipper "in particular, is a gathering place for homosexuals of both sexes, as well as other vice characters."

A follow-up November 1962 FBI memo expanded membership in the homosexual crowd from the "list of 176 males" to between three and four hundred members, and identified the additional premises: The Royal Lanai; Golden B Bar, on Kapiolani; The Glade on North Hotel Street, downtown Honolulu; The Chinatown Grill, downtown Honolulu; Happy Saimin Stand, North Hotel Street; A-1 Bakery, Beretania and Aala Lane; and Ledi's Hotel, above the Shanty Bar on Smith Street.

A March 1962 FBI memo implicated some individuals from the gay crowd in the prostitution rackets and drug culture:

[Redacted], Waikiki – A jazz club catering to Negroes and vice characters. [Redacted] described as a known homosexual, is manager.

[Redacted], is a suspected dope addict, as is the doorman, [redacted] and [redacted] who have been appearing as entertainers, are suspected Lesbians and conduct some prostitution activities on a limited scale. Waitress [redacted] and two others, names unknown, are also suspected prostitutes and dope addicts. Honolulu [informant], on February 1, 1962, reported that [redacted] and [redacted] partners with a Chinese woman in operation of the [redacted] are both homosexuals. On February 23, 1962, [informant] reported that [redacted] is now appearing at "The Little Dipper" in Waikiki and [redacted] is appearing at the Beachwalk Inn.

The gay scene on the islands alarmed the Hawaii State Commission on Children and Youth which "appointed a study committee to inquire into the homosexual situation as it might affect children and youth, and corrective steps which might be taken to avoid its development in youth."

Up the Pacific coast in the Northwest a gay bar in Seattle, Washington attracted a party 'n play element. In 1951 police arrested four men from a dive establishment in the Skidroad section for allegedly distributing amphetamine sulfate according to the 1956 testimony of Kenneth Monfore, the FDA Chief for the Seattle District, before a

Congressional committee. Monfore testified that "the four arrested were known to the police as confirmed homosexual," and they were apprehended after police detectives "dressed themselves in the type clothing common to that of the homosexual crowd and frequented the Skidroad tavern where, according to information obtained, these drugs were being promiscuously distributed." Although the undercover investigation "did not directly disclose that these dangerous drugs were being sold or distributed to juveniles, our inspectors did observe that juveniles were hanging around the outside of the tavern in question and on occasion the juveniles left the area accompanied by one of the known homosexuals."

The Southwest experienced an influx of gays and lesbians in the late 1950s. For example, the Phoenix Police Department Vice Squad Commander advised "that during the winter of 1957 and 1958, there was a marked increase in the number of homosexuals both male and female coming to Phoenix" according to a May 1958 FBI report:

He stated that this apparently is the result of the lax Arizona laws concerning the control of these individuals. [Redacted] pointed out that many complaints are received by his department about these people but very little can be done by his department merely because these people have a peculiar look or outlook. He stated that actually they must be caught in indecent acts probably in a public place or in the presence of juveniles before a successful prosecution could result.

The vice cop thought enacting laws against cross-dressing might help to resolve the supposed problem:

[Redacted] pointed out transvestitism is not in itself in violation of the law in Arizona as it is in other places and that possibly a law against that would help curb the activity of both lesbians and male homosexuals. [Redacted] said he of course realized the difficulties of framing a law of such nature as applies to females due to their present accepted habit of wearing male clothing even in decent society.

The "Captain's Table, a tavern at 5338 North 7th Street, Phoenix, is a hangout for homosexuals, both male and female," and "Kay's Happy Landing, a tavern at Central and Broadway, in Phoenix, and the Rocking Horse Tavern, 24th Avenue and Glenrosa, are also hangouts for homosexuals, principally females."

In New Mexico the "Santa Fe Police Department has advised that the most notorious place of amusement is Claude's Restaurant and Bar, located at 840 Canyon Road," and this establishment allegedly caters to Lesbians, and homosexuals, as well as other 'arty and Bohemian type' individuals" according to a March 1958 FBI memo. Meanwhile, in Albuquerque a police commander "stated that he had gotten reports that homosexuals were frequenting Smitty's Hideway Bar on the corner of Central and Seventh Street, N.W., in the downtown area, and his undercover officers had reported that there appeared to be several individuals who might be homosexuals hanging around the bar" according to an October 1958 FBI memo. Apparently the bar's owner "in the past . . . had been very uncooperative with the police in reporting matters that should have been reported."

In the Midwest the FBI noted numerous gay bars in its files during the late 1950s. The FBI identified two gay bars in Minneapolis, Minnesota: "'queers' frequent the Pit Barbeque and the Dugout." In St. Louis, Missouri the "bars most frequented by homosexuals, according to the Vice Squad, are Chapnick's Bar, 620 Pine, and Shelly's Midway Bar, 3528 Olive Street." In nearby Collinsville, Illinois the Candlelight Club was once "a hangout for ex-convicts and local police characters" but "recently has become a 'lesbian' hangout." The FBI documented only one gay bar in Akron, Ohio:

"The Lincoln Bar, S. Howard Street, Akron, continues to attract homosexuals and sex deviates, but is frequently checked by the Akron Police Department Vice Squad and there has been no indication of important criminal elements gathering there, nor has there been any indication of illegal activity of any type there."

Given the mob entrenchment in Midwest cities the FBI not surprisingly alleged Mafia connections to some of the gay bars. Carmen Basile, a made guy in the Cleveland Mafia, ran Rinnella's Bar at East 65th and Carnegie Avenue which was a hoodlum meeting place during the week but on Friday and Saturday nights was "a hangout of Lesbians" according to a March 1958 FBI memo. Basile worked under mob capo Frank Brancato, and "made a statement to an Agent of the Cleveland Office to the effect that he had high respect for FRANK BRANCATO and if he had a son he would like the boy to model himself after BRANCATO."

The FBI identified the following "homosexual hangouts" in Milwaukee, Wisconsin in a 1959 memo: The Clifton Bar at 336 West Juneau; The Royal Hotel Bar at 5th and Michigan Street; The White Horse Inn at 1426 North 11th Street; The Riviera Bar at 401 North Plankington Avenue; and The Wildwood Bar, a "colored lesbian hangout," at 1420

West Walnut Street. Apparently it was necessary for gay bars to have the "proper protection" – i.e., making payoffs – in order to operate without police raids.

One gay bar which did not have the "proper protection" was the Pink Glove at 631 North Broadway according to a July 1958 FBI file concerning its closure by Milwaukee cops:

> Information has been developed that the "Pink Glove" Cocktail Lounge has had its license revoked by the Milwaukee PD because it has gained the reputation of being a "fag" hangout; that is, being patronized by queers and sex perverts. This cocktail lounge was licensed to [name redacted] although it is believed that [name redacted] had a financial interest in it. The cocktail lounge is now "for sale" and [name redacted] owner of the popular Jordan's Restaurant on North Water Street, is believed to be interested in purchasing it. Jordan's Restaurant caters to the sporting crowd on Milwaukee's financial row - North Water Street. [Name redacted] has been heard to have said that the reason the Milwaukee PD closed the "Pink Glove" is because he did not have the proper "protection."

The watering hole did not have a long life as a gay

bar. The license holder for the Pink Glove was Marvin Klein, and it previously had operated as Phillips Cocktail Lounge. However, according to FBI files, "this cocktail lounge was recently leased or in some manner the [name redacted] took in partners who are homosexuals with the resultant change in the name of the cocktail lounge to the Pink Glove, which in a matter of weeks became so notorious as a hangout for homosexuals in Milwaukee that the Milwaukee Police Department has been literally forced to close the place up."

Marvin's two brothers Harold and Bernard were suspected racketeers with various interests in coin-operated machines, waste carting and salvage, and bars and booze, and had alleged ties to reputed hoodlums including the DiMaggio brothers, Isadore Pogrob and Jack Enea. Even in Brew City the underworld was a violent life. Enea was gunned down in November 1955, and Pogrob gunned down in January 1960. Notwithstanding some suspicion about their dealings the Klein brothers never were convicted of any crimes. Harold and Bernard were charged in 1962 of receiving stolen property but acquitted amid accusations of intimidating a prosecution witness.

The FBI stated in a 1958 memo that mob boss Frank Balistrieri may have a hidden interest in the Pink Glove:

FRANK BALISTRIERI is alleged to have an interest in the "Pink Glove," which is newly opened, a cocktail lounge at 631 North Broadway, and which is operated by [name redacted]. An informant has advised that he has seen an employee of FRANK BALISTRIERI's observe the activities at the "Pink Glove" cocktail lounge and check the cash register and report his findings back to FRANK BALISTRIERI. The informant advised he had no information which indicated that this "Pink Glove" cocktail lounge was a part of a country operation which catered to the "gay crowd." A "gay crowd" is described as individuals who participate in various acts of sexual perversion. It was the understanding of this informant that the "Pink Glove" may be a name used to designate a certain spot in various parts of the country where gay crowds meet.

The FBI alleged that Balistrieri also had interests in straight bars including "the Roosevelt Bar, the Melody Room, the Downtowner Bar, the Tradewinds Lounge and the Knights Tower Bar, all in the city of Milwaukee."

The FBI documents surveying gay bars throughout the United States found remarkably few in New England. In a 1958 memo the FBI noted the following in Hartford, Connecticut: Five O'clock Club at 144 Front Street ("recently this club had initiated a policy of entertainment and was catering to perverts"); Peerless Restaurant at 189 Main Street ("frequented by sex deviates, mainly 'queers'"); and The Men's Bar at the Garde Hotel at 366 Asylum Street ("frequented by 'queers'").

The FBI also reported man-on-man action at Fort Devens, Massachusetts. Fort Devens was a permanent installation in nearby Ayers with fifteen thousand Army soldiers, and military officials had "secured evidence of homosexual activities by 21 soldiers":

> Some of these activities have been with civilians off post. [Redacted] Provost Marshal of Fort Devens, has stated that on numerous occasions the contacts with civilian homosexuals have been made at the Chatterbox, a tavern located in the town of Ayer approximately one mile from Fort Devens. There is no information to show that any illegal activity ever took place within this tavern. The Army took "appropriate disciplinary action . . . in all cases," and "information relating to these contacts as known to the Army is being

made available to the Chief of Police and the Town Selectmen, who are responsible for the issuance of liquor licenses in Ayer."

A subsequent update advised that by November 1958 the homosexual problem was eliminated: "The Chatterbox at Ayer, Massachusetts, adjacent to Fort Devens, Massachusetts, was reported in the past to be a meeting spot for homosexuals, both civilian and military. Vigorous policing by both the Ayer police and the Military police has eliminated this problem in the past three months." However, the FBI would remain vigilant, and stated that "Fort Devens, Massachusetts, continues to be the scene of regular investigative activity of this investigative agency" with "regular and willing cooperation . . . from the Provost Marshal and the men in his command."

The FBI found lots of gay action in the Northeast states of New York and Pennsylvania. Manhattan may have had the most fabulous gay bars in the late 1950s but queens on Long Island and in the outer boros did not have to schlep into the city for a night out. Many gay bars existed during the late 1950s in small Long Island towns including "the following locations from time to time cater to homosexuals of both sexes": Red Door, 167 New Hyde Park Road, Franklin Square; The C'est Bon, 2520 Merrick Road, Belmore, New York; The West

Park Inn, 157 Hempstead Avenue, West Hempstead, New York; and Farina's, Hempstead Turnpike, Elmont, New York. The FBI "noted that [name redacted] has been generally conceded to be the 'queen bee' among homosexuals in the Nassau County area, and formerly operated out of the West Park Inn, West Hempstead, New York" which was "a 'queer' hangout . . . frequented by local college students." The FBI further "noted that during 1959 The Red Door, Franklin Square, New York and Farina's closed."

North of Long Island in Newburgh, NY was Stewart Air Force Base, and the base's Provost Marshal reported to the FBI that "he has had a number of complaints, about several bars in the city" including Andy's at 199 Chambers Street "which he said is a hangout for male deviates with a floor show composed of a number of female impersonators" and Luke's at 40 Chambers Street which "he said is catering to a number of Lesbians."

On Staten Island an informant advised the FBI that the Mayfair Tavern at 3 Hyatt Street "continues to be a hangout for homosexuals" and "CARMEN's tavern is a known hangout for homosexuals and perverts." Mount Vernon in Westchester County borders the Bronx, and the FBI did not identify any gay bars there but observed "the Arcade Bowling

Alleys, 44 South 3rd Avenue and the Mount Vernon Arena, a roller-skating rink, at 240 West Lincoln are reputedly known hangouts for perverts."

Gays and lesbians were finding their community in small towns and big cities across Pennsylvania in the late 1950s. In a March 31, 1958 memo the FBI identified the following establishments in Philadelphia at which there was "the activity or prevalence of homosexuals": Wagon Wheel Cafe, 11th Street, below Spruce; Family Theater, 1313 Market Street; Allegro Bar, 1412 Spruce Street; Forrest Bar, 204 South Quince Street; The Hideaway, 1301 Locust Street; Maxine's Bar, 243 South Camac Street; Pirate Ship, 210 South Camac Street; and Surf Club, 1329 Manning Street. All of these gay bars except for Family Theater were "located on the Locust-Spruce Streets night club area of center-city Philadelphia."

It wasn't just in the City of Brotherly Love where the gays gathered together according to a series of FBI memos from the late 1950s. The Lark Hotel on DeKalb Street in Bridgeport was "a favorite hangout for lesbians of the area," and during the summer there was an influx of homosexual actors into New Hope who performed at the "Bucks County Playhouse which puts on summer stock plays," and their favorite "hangouts" were the Canal

House and the Black Bass Hotel. A popular gay bar in Lancaster, Pennsylvania was The Village at 28 East Chestnut Street owned and managed by Peter Photis which had a bar, night club and cellar cafe:

> The Village engaged floor shows in which nudity and smutty jokes were the centers of attraction. As a result of complaints and repeated attendance at the floor shows by members of the Lancaster Police Department sufficient information was obtained without getting enough evidence for criminal prosecution so that PHOTIS was ordered by Police authorities to either clean up the floor shows or face arrest. PHOTIS cleaned up the floor shows. In a conversation with PHOTIS on May 4, 1959, PHOTIS advised SA PHILIP M. CULLEN that the cellar cafe is a hangout for "queers," and that he had discovered that one of his bartenders in the cafe was "queer." PHOTIS said that he had fired the bartender but did not know how to rid the place of the remaining "queers" and would probably continue to let them into the cafe.

Other Pennsylvania spots identified by the FBI were Andy's Musical Bar, 2336 West Third Street, Chester, which was "a hangout for perverts and frequently has female impersonators in the show," and the Circle Bar owned by Matt Whitaker at 118

East Norwegian Street, Pottsville, which was "the meeting place for homosexuals and perverts."

Gay men were finding each other during the late 1950s even in the South according to FBI files. In Macon, Georgia "nightclubs frequented by homosexuals" were identified as Ann's Tic Toc Tavern and The Tropic Bar and Grill. The "main spot of congregations for homosexuals in the vicinity of Raleigh, North Carolina, continued to be the Kitty Hawk Tavern of the Hotel Sir Walter and at Player's Retreat, 2808 Hillsboro Street." In Fort Smith, Arkansas "The Cozy Corner, 2200 Midland Boulevard, has been noted to be the 'hangout' of numerous persons suspected of being sexual perverts." The FBI identified several places in Little Rock "considered to be notorious in that persons of ill repute such as prostitutes, procurers, alcoholics, and sex deviates appear to frequent" them but did not specifically identify which crowd was patronizing what bar. Apparently there was plenty of gay action in the men's room at the Continental Bus Terminal in Memphis, Tennessee – a "hangout for queers" as reflected by an August 1959 FBI report: "since January 1, 1959, over 200 men have been arrested at this rest room who were involved in homosexuality."

The FBI identified "three principal areas of the city of New Orleans where notorious places of amusement are located" in a March 21, 1958 memo:

> The New Orleans French Quarter, the Canal Street area, in the vicinity of the Jung Hotel, the 1300 to the 1900 block, and St. Charles Street, from the 500 block to the 1400 block. These three areas contain numerous barrooms and taverns which feature strip-tease dancers, B-drinkers, and offer opportunities for prostitutes to congregate.

Of course, these areas included gay bars such as "Cy's Bar, in the 500 block of Esplanade Avenue, operated by CYRUS MELITO, which is frequented by prostitutes as well as being a notorious hangout for homosexuals."

However, the gay fun in the Big Easy took a big hit when "the New Orleans Police Department, in the spring of 1959, began an all-out campaign to reduce the number of sex deviates, and has forced such night clubs as Tony Bacino's and Cy's Bar to close" as reported in September 1959 by the FBI:

> Both barrooms were notorious hangouts for the exhibitionist type sex deviates, and were a continuous source of trouble. This action has caused a number of the notorious sex deviates to leave the city of New Orleans. At the present time, the My-O-My Club, located in Jefferson Parish, is the only night club featuring female

impersonators and the management of this club is most careful to keep deviates from hanging out in this club. The My-O-My Club is now a tourist attraction and visited regularly by the various sightseeing buses.

The FBI files from the late 1950s and early 1960s disclose a number of gay bars operating across the Sunshine State. In Jacksonville, Florida the FBI found Smitty's Beach Club on First Avenue was "frequented by prostitutes on holiday and queers," the Mayfair Bar on Beach Boulevard was a "hangout for queers," and Millie's Bar was "frequented by prostitutes and sex perverts." In Tampa the FBI identified Jimmy White's Tavern at 1725 Grand Central Avenue and Knotty Pine Bar at 723 Morgan Street as "hangouts for homosexuals."

In Miami the FBI named several gay bars including a few which were operated by reputed mobster Pete Arnstein a/k/a Pete Arnold from Chicago who also allegedly was involved with burglary crews and the flesh trade. Arnstein's gay bars were identified as the Pin Up Bar at 2228 Park Avenue and the Jamaica Cocktail Lounge at the Kingston Hotel, and were described as rather seedy. The "Pin-Up Bar in Miami Beach a hangout for narcotics users, unsavory characters and homosexuals," and "a hangout for questionable male individuals and narcotics pushers," and at the Jamaica Cocktail Lounge "a number of hoodlums . . . hang out at this bar as well as homosexuals."

Arnstein was an alleged associate of Joseph Sonken who owned the Gold Coast Restaurant and Lounge in Hollywood, Florida which apparently was used as "a Mafia meeting place" since its opening in 1948, and "investigators also have said the restaurant was used as a national relay center for organized crime families that wanted to pass messages to one another" including Gambino boss John Gotti as reported by Mike Billington in a June 3, 1990 obituary on Sonken for the *Sun-Sentinel*. Chicago police claimed Sonken and Arnstein were involved with a "major prostitution ring," and in Miami Sonken and Arnstein's wife allegedly operated the Mother Kelly's nightclub at 1405 Dade Boulevard. Arnstein also was behind the Mayflower Lounge strip joint at 1716 Alton Road, and owned the Indian Creek Apartments at 5970 Indian Creek Drive according to FBI files.

Other gay bars in Miami during the later 1950s were The Left Bank which was "a new Lesbian establishment . . . in the rear of the Chez Joey Night Club" at 829 Biscayne Boulevard, and the Exclusive Club at 3661 Southwest 8th Street. The FBI files indicate an unspecified tie between Chez Joey and the Exclusive Club although it is unclear whether there was a common ownership as the names are redacted. One informant advised that "the Exclusive Club caters to queers and lesbians." Another informant related the Exclusive Club "is frequented by homosexuals," and apparently paying off a "'bagman' for the Miami Police Department in the district in which this club is located."

Fifty years ago the principal haven for LGBT folks was a bar subculture, and due to the illicit status of such establishments it is astounding how pervasive they were in far-flung places across the United States. There is little public record of their existence, and thanks only to a snooping FBI in concert with local police has their history been preserved. Sadly, perhaps the best sources for LGBT history may be local law enforcement agencies keeping tabs on the sexual outlaws, and to fully reclaim this past their records need to be obtained through state FOIA requests.

ABOUT THE AUTHOR

Phillip Crawford Jr. is a retired attorney from the New York bar. He attended Bates College in Lewiston, Maine from which he graduated with a B.A. in English in 1985. At Bates he was President of the Gay-Straight Alliance, and in 1983 spearheaded a campaign to oust military recruiters from the campus for their discriminatory policies against the LGBT community. He attended George Washington University Law School where he was a Notes Editor for the *Law Review*. After graduating with highest honors as class salutatorian in 1988 he clerked for Chief Judge Judith W. Rogers on the District of Columbia Court of Appeals, and then with Judge George H. Revercomb on the United States District Court for the District of Columbia. He practiced law for fifteen years in New York City including several years with the plaintiffs' class action bar, and then retired after exposing his concerns about billing practices. Professor Lester Brickman characterized him in *Lawyer Barons* as a "whistle blower." Crawford also is the author of *The Mafia and the Gays* (2015) and *Railroaded: The Homophobic Prosecution of Brandon Woodruff for His Parents' Murders* (2018).